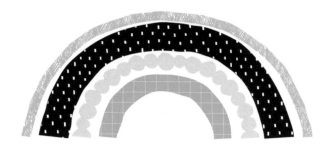

PRESENTED TO:

....

FROM:

....

DATE:

....

THE BIBLE PROMISE BOOK®

for

TEEN GIRLS

BARBOUR
PUBLISHING

Published by Barbour Publishing, Inc., 1810 Barbour Drive, Uhrichsville, Ohio 44683, www.barbourbooks.com

Our mission is to inspire the world with the life-changing message of the Bible.

ecpa Member of the Evangelical Christian Publishers Association

Printed in China.

CONTENTS

INTRODUCTION

When you're a teenager, life stretches ahead like a super-highway of opportunity. Your options are (almost) limitless—but there will also be bumps and detours along the way. Whatever direction you choose to take with your life, it's important to keep your head and your heart focused on God and His Word.

That's what *The Bible Promise Book for Teen Girls* is all about. This collection of scriptures will give you the best guidance on the *real* issues of life—the things that matter most! You'll find forty-one, important-to-you topics, each followed by ultimate truth from God's unchanging Word. Brief introductions and thought-provoking quotations enhance each section, making this a book you'll return to for years to come.

We hope *The Bible Promise Book for Teen Girls* will always point you toward the one Book that *is* truth—the Bible. With God's Word as your guide, you'll be on your way to a fantastic future!

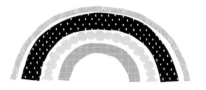

ADVERSITY

One of Satan's biggest lies is that the Christian life should be free from adversity. The longer you live, the more you'll realize that adversity is the rule in life, not the exception. But don't look at problems as things to be avoided: these are the times that test your character, patience, and faith. Sure, we might suffer grief and pain, but with Christ, we can endure any hardship. Hey, Job lost everything—but he still gave glory to God.

The LORD also will be a refuge for the oppressed,
a refuge in times of trouble. And those who know
Your name will put their trust in You; for You,
LORD, have not forsaken those who seek You.
PSALM 9:9–10 NKJV

. . .

After you have suffered for a little while, the God of all
grace, who called you to His eternal glory in Christ, will
Himself perfect, confirm, strengthen and establish you.
1 PETER 5:10 NASB

. . .

For even Christ did not please himself but, as it is
written: "The insults of those who insult you have fallen
on me." For everything that was written in the past was
written to teach us, so that through endurance and the
encouragement of the Scriptures we might have hope.
ROMANS 15:3–4 NIV

. . .

"Come to Me, all you who labor and are heavy laden,
and I will give you rest. Take My yoke upon you
and learn from Me, for I am gentle and lowly in heart,
and you will find rest for your souls. For My yoke
is easy and My burden is light."
MATTHEW 11:28–30 NKJV

"When you pass through the waters, I will be with you; and through the rivers, they will not overflow you. When you walk through the fire, you will not be scorched, nor will the flame burn you."
ISAIAH 43:2 NASB

. . .

Are any among you suffering? They should keep on praying about it. And those who have reason to be thankful should continually sing praises to the Lord.
JAMES 5:13 NLT

. . .

If you are reproached for the name of Christ, blessed are you, for the Spirit of glory and of God rests upon you. On their part He is blasphemed, but on your part He is glorified.
1 PETER 4:14 NKJV

. . .

For the Lord will not reject forever, for if He causes grief, then He will have compassion according to His abundant lovingkindness.
LAMENTATIONS 3:31–32 NASB

Even though I walk through the valley of the
shadow of death, I fear no evil, for You are with me;
Your rod and Your staff, they comfort me.
PSALM 23:4 NASB

. . .

For as the sufferings of Christ abound in us, so our
consolation also aboundeth by Christ. And whether we
be afflicted, it is for your consolation and salvation, which
is effectual in the enduring of the same sufferings which
we also suffer: or whether we be comforted, it is for your
consolation and salvation. And our hope of you is stedfast,
knowing, that as ye are partakers of the sufferings,
so shall ye be also of the consolation.
2 CORINTHIANS 1:5–7 KJV

. . .

. . .but rejoice to the extent that you partake
of Christ's sufferings, that when His glory is revealed,
you may also be glad with exceeding joy.
1 PETER 4:13 NKJV

. . .

Record my lament; list my tears on your scroll—are they
not in your record? Then my enemies will turn back when
I call for help. By this I will know that God is for me.
PSALM 56:8–9 NIV

Do not fear any of those things which you are about to suffer. Indeed, the devil is about to throw some of you into prison, that you may be tested, and you will have tribulation ten days. Be faithful until death, and I will give you the crown of life.

REVELATION 2:10 NKJV

• • •

For this finds favor, if for the sake of conscience toward God a person bears up under sorrows when suffering unjustly. For what credit is there if, when you sin and are harshly treated, you endure it with patience? But if when you do what is right and suffer for it you patiently endure it, this finds favor with God. For you have been called for this purpose, since Christ also suffered for you, leaving you an example for you to follow in His steps, "Who committed no sin, nor was any deceit found in his mouth"; and while being reviled, He did not revile in return; while suffering, He uttered no threats, but kept entrusting Himself to Him who judges righteously.

1 PETER 2:19–23 NASB

• • •

He will swallow up death forever! The Sovereign LORD will wipe away all tears. He will remove forever all insults and mockery against his land and people. The LORD has spoken!

ISAIAH 25:8 NLT

Casting all your care upon Him, for He cares for you.
1 PETER 5:7 NKJV

. . .

And lest I should be exalted above measure through
the abundance of the revelations, there was given to me
a thorn in the flesh, the messenger of Satan to buffet me,
lest I should be exalted above measure. For this thing I
besought the Lord thrice, that it might depart from me.
And he said unto me, My grace is sufficient for thee:
for my strength is made perfect in weakness. Most
gladly therefore will I rather glory in my infirmities,
that the power of Christ may rest upon me.
2 CORINTHIANS 12:7–9 KJV

. . .

The LORD is good, a stronghold in the day of
trouble; and He knows those who trust in Him.
NAHUM 1:7 NKJV

. . .

"Blessed are you who hunger now, for you shall be
satisfied. Blessed are you who weep now, for you shall
laugh. Blessed are you when men hate you, and ostracize
you, and insult you, and scorn your name as evil, for the
sake of the Son of Man. Be glad in that day and leap for
joy, for behold, your reward is great in heaven. For in the
same way their fathers used to treat the prophets."
LUKE 6:21–23 NASB

Weeping may remain for a night,
but rejoicing comes in the morning.
PSALM 30:5 NIV

. . .

Blessed is the man who endures temptation; for when
he has been approved, he will receive the crown of life
which the Lord has promised to those who love Him.
JAMES 1:12 NKJV

. . .

Rejoicing in hope, persevering
in tribulation, devoted to prayer. . .
ROMANS 12:12 NASB

. . .

"I have told you all this so that you may have peace in me.
Here on earth you will have many trials and sorrows.
But take heart, because I have overcome the world."
JOHN 16:33 NLT

. . .

"Blessed are those who mourn,
for they shall be comforted."
MATTHEW 5:4 NKJV

. . .

The righteous cry out, and the LORD hears,
and delivers them out of all their troubles.
PSALM 34:17 NKJV

In this you greatly rejoice, even though now for a little while, if necessary, you have been distressed by various trials, so that the proof of your faith, being more precious than gold which is perishable, even though tested by fire, may be found to result in praise and glory and honor at the revelation of Jesus Christ.

1 PETER 1:6–7 NASB

• • •

For our light affliction, which is but
for a moment, worketh for us a far more
exceeding and eternal weight of glory.

2 CORINTHIANS 4:17 KJV

• • •

For I consider that the sufferings of this
present time are not worthy to be compared
with the glory that is to be revealed to us.

ROMANS 8:18 NASB

When everything seems to be going
against you, remember that the airplane
takes off against the wind, not with it.

HENRY FORD

ANGER

You've probably heard the old saying, "Don't get mad, get even." Well, here's some good advice for you: Don't do either. Anger robs people of the joy of the Christian life. On the other hand, being quick to forgive will help you defeat those angry feelings. Ask God for His strength to swap your anger for His joy.

My dear brothers, take note of this: Everyone
should be quick to listen, slow to speak and slow to
become angry, for man's anger does not bring
about the righteous life that God desires.
JAMES 1:19–20 NIV

. . .

Do not associate with a man given to anger;
or go with a hot-tempered man, or you will
learn his ways and find a snare for yourself.
PROVERBS 22:24–25 NASB

. . .

Don't be quick-tempered, for anger is the friend of fools.
ECCLESIASTES 7:9 NLT

. . .

The discretion of a man makes him slow to anger,
and his glory is to overlook a transgression.
PROVERBS 19:11 NKJV

. . .

A man of great wrath will suffer punishment.
PROVERBS 19:19 NKJV

. . .

"Be angry, and yet do not sin"; do not let the sun
go down on your anger, and do not give the devil
an opportunity. . . . Let all bitterness and wrath
and anger and clamor and slander be put
away from you, along with all malice.
EPHESIANS 4:26–27, 31 NASB

A fool's wrath is presently known:
but a prudent man covereth shame.
PROVERBS 12:16 KJV

• • •

For wrath kills a foolish man, and envy slays a simple one.
JOB 5:2 NKJV

• • •

Do all things without grumbling or disputing.
PHILIPPIANS 2:14 NASB

• • •

Starting a quarrel is like breaching a dam;
so drop the matter before a dispute breaks out.
PROVERBS 17:14 NIV

• • •

"But I say to you that whoever is angry with
his brother without a cause shall be in danger of
the judgment. And whoever says to his brother, 'Raca!'
shall be in danger of the council. But whoever says,
'You fool!' shall be in danger of hell fire."
MATTHEW 5:22 NKJV

• • •

Dear friends, never avenge yourselves. Leave
that to God. For it is written, "I will take vengeance;
I will repay those who deserve it," says the Lord.
ROMANS 12:19 NLT

A man of great wrath will suffer punishment;
Cease from anger and forsake wrath;
do not fret; it leads only to evildoing.
PSALM 37:8 NASB

. . .

He that is soon angry dealeth foolishly. . . .
He that is slow to wrath is of great understanding:
but he that is hasty of spirit exalteth folly.
PROVERBS 14:17, 29 KJV

. . .

But now you yourselves are to put off
all these: anger, wrath, malice, blasphemy,
filthy language out of your mouth.
COLOSSIANS 3:8 NKJV

. . .

A gentle answer turns away wrath, but a harsh
word stirs up anger. . . . A hot-tempered man stirs
up strife, but the slow to anger calms a dispute.
PROVERBS 15:1, 18 NASB

For every minute you are angry,
you lose sixty seconds of happiness.
RALPH WALDO EMERSON

CONVERSATION

Like a comic book superhero, you possess an amazing power—the words you say. With words, you can affect another person's life dramatically—in either a positive or a negative way. Think hard about the words you say before you say them; unlike computer files, those words can't be deleted once they've been spoken. Make it a point always to speak positively—words of kindness, helpfulness, and mercy. Use your "power" for good!

When words are many, sin is not
absent, but he who holds his tongue is wise.
PROVERBS 10:19 NIV

. . .

"A good man out of the good treasure of his heart brings
forth good things, and an evil man out of the evil treasure
brings forth evil things. But I say to you that for every idle
word men may speak, they will give account of it in the
day of judgment. For by your words you will be justified,
and by your words you will be condemned."
MATTHEW 12:35–37 NKJV

. . .

A man has joy in an apt answer,
and how delightful is a timely word!
PROVERBS 15:23 NASB

. . .

For the Scriptures say, "If you want a happy life and
good days, keep your tongue from speaking evil,
and keep your lips from telling lies."
1 PETER 3:10 NLT

. . .

Do not speak evil of one another, brethren.
He who speaks evil of a brother and judges his brother,
speaks evil of the law and judges the law. But if you
judge the law, you are not a doer of the law but a judge.
JAMES 4:11 NKJV

Let your speech always be with grace,
as though seasoned with salt, so that you will
know how you should respond to each person.
COLOSSIANS 4:6 NASB

•   •   •

Set a watch, O LORD, before my mouth;
keep the door of my lips.
PSALM 141:3 KJV

•   •   •

A fool vents all his feelings,
but a wise man holds them back.
PROVERBS 29:11 NKJV

•   •   •

If anyone thinks himself to be religious,
and yet does not bridle his tongue but deceives
his own heart, this man's religion is worthless.
JAMES 1:26 NASB

•   •   •

He who guards his mouth and his
tongue keeps himself from calamity.
PROVERBS 21:23 NIV

•   •   •

Let no corrupt word proceed out of your mouth,
but what is good for necessary edification,
that it may impart grace to the hearers.
EPHESIANS 4:29 NKJV

For we all stumble in many ways. If anyone does not stumble in what he says, he is a perfect man, able to bridle the whole body as well. Now if we put the bits into the horses' mouths so that they will obey us, we direct their entire body as well. Look at the ships also, though they are so great and are driven by strong winds, are still directed by a very small rudder wherever the inclination of the pilot desires. So also the tongue is a small part of the body, and yet it boasts of great things. See how great a forest is set aflame by such a small fire! And the tongue is a fire, the very world of iniquity; the tongue is set among our members as that which defiles the entire body, and sets on fire the course of our life, and is set on fire by hell. For every species of beasts and birds, of reptiles and creatures of the sea, is tamed and has been tamed by the human race. But no one can tame the tongue; it is a restless evil and full of deadly poison. With it we bless our Lord and Father, and with it we curse men, who have been made in the likeness of God; from the same mouth come both blessing and cursing. My brethren, these things ought not to be this way.

JAMES 3:2–10 NASB

• • •

But now ye also put off all these; anger, wrath, malice, blasphemy, filthy communication out of your mouth.

COLOSSIANS 3:8 KJV

Do you see a man hasty in his words?
There is more hope for a fool than for him.
PROVERBS 29:20 NKJV

• • •

"When they bring you before the synagogues and
the rulers and the authorities, do not worry about
how or what you are to speak in your defense,
or what you are to say; for the Holy Spirit will teach
you in that very hour what you ought to say."
LUKE 12:11–12 NASB

• • •

I said, "I will watch my ways and keep my tongue
from sin; I will put a muzzle on my mouth as
long as the wicked are in my presence."
PSALM 39:1 NIV

• • •

But above all, my brethren, do not swear, either by heaven
or by earth or with any other oath. But let your "Yes,"
be "Yes," and your "No," "No," lest you fall into judgment.
JAMES 5:12 NKJV

Kind words can be short and easy to speak,
but their echoes are truly endless.
MOTHER TERESA

COUNSEL

Who you gonna listen to? Modern society, through TV, movies, and music, will give you plenty of advice—most of it bad. Taking counsel from God and committed Christians, though, will provide an entirely different perspective—the right one. Choose to follow God's counsel. He is perfect and has laid out clear instructions to obey in His Word, the Bible. He'll also use other Christians to help guide you in the decisions that you must make—and you'll have plenty.

The way of a fool is right in his own eyes,
but a wise man is he who listens to counsel.
PROVERBS 12:15 NASB

. . .

Then Jehoshaphat added, "But first let's
find out what the LORD says."
1 KINGS 22:5 NLT

. . .

For unto us a Child is born, unto us a Son is given;
and the government will be upon His shoulder. And His
name will be called Wonderful, Counselor.
ISAIAH 9:6 NKJV

. . .

Listen to counsel and accept discipline,
that you may be wise the rest of your days.
PROVERBS 19:20 NASB

. . .

Howbeit when he, the Spirit of truth, is come,
he will guide you into all truth: for he shall not speak
of himself; but whatsoever he shall hear, that shall
he speak: and he will shew you things to come.
JOHN 16:13 KJV

. . .

All your children shall be taught by the LORD,
and great shall be the peace of your children.
ISAIAH 54:13 NKJV

All discipline for the moment seems not to be joyful,
but sorrowful; yet to those who have been trained by it,
afterwards it yields the peaceful fruit of righteousness.
HEBREWS 12:11 NASB

. . .

Instruct a wise man and he will be wiser still; teach
a righteous man and he will add to his learning.
PROVERBS 9:9 NIV

. . .

Brethren, if a man is overtaken in any trespass, you who
are spiritual restore such a one in a spirit of gentleness,
considering yourself lest you also be tempted.
GALATIANS 6:1 NKJV

. . .

They should gently teach those who oppose
the truth. Perhaps God will change those people's
hearts, and they will believe the truth.
2 TIMOTHY 2:25 NLT

. . .

"With Him are wisdom and strength,
He has counsel and understanding."
JOB 12:13 NKJV

Oil and perfume make the heart glad,
so a man's counsel is sweet to his friend.
PROVERBS 27:9 NASB

• • •

I will instruct thee and teach thee in the way which
thou shalt go: I will guide thee with mine eye.
PSALM 32:8 KJV

• • •

And those of the people who
understand shall instruct many.
DANIEL 11:33 NKJV

• • •

Where there is no guidance the people fall,
but in abundance of counselors there is victory.
PROVERBS 11:14 NASB

• • •

The Spirit of the LORD will rest on him—the Spirit of
wisdom and of understanding, the Spirit of counsel and of
power, the Spirit of knowledge and of the fear of the LORD.
ISAIAH 11:2 NIV

• • •

Blessed is the man who walks not in the counsel
of the ungodly, nor stands in the path of sinners,
nor sits in the seat of the scornful.
PSALM 1:1 NKJV

Without consultation, plans are frustrated,
but with many counselors they succeed.
PROVERBS 15:22 NASB

. . .

The LORD Almighty is a wonderful teacher,
and he gives the farmer great wisdom.

ISAIAH 28:29 NLT

. . .

You will guide me with Your counsel,
and afterward receive me to glory.
PSALM 73:24 NKJV

. . .

A wise man will hear and increase in learning,
and a man of understanding will acquire wise counsel.
PROVERBS 1:5 NASB

Appreciate the commands of
scripture as much as the promises.
BRUCE & STAN

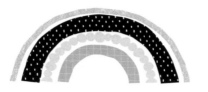

COURAGE

Courage isn't skiing down the vertical face of a mountain, one step ahead of an advancing avalanche. (*Crazy,* maybe.) Courage is doing the right thing, even when "the right thing" scares you. You'll have to make many decisions in life. Resolve today that, with God's help, you will have the courage to make the right choices—every time.

So that we may boldly say, The Lord is my helper,
and I will not fear what man shall do unto me.
HEBREWS 13:6 KJV

. . .

For God has not given us a spirit of fear,
but of power and of love and of a sound mind.
2 TIMOTHY 1:7 NKJV

. . .

By this, love is perfected with us, so that we
may have confidence in the day of judgment;
because as He is, so also are we in this world.
1 JOHN 4:17 NASB

. . .

Whatever happens, conduct yourselves in a manner
worthy of the gospel of Christ. Then, whether I come
and see you or only hear about you in my absence,
I will know that you stand firm in one spirit, contending
as one man for the faith of the gospel without being
frightened in any way by those who oppose you.
This is a sign to them that they will be destroyed,
but that you will be saved—and that by God.
PHILIPPIANS 1:27–28 NIV

In the fear of the LORD there is strong confidence,
and His children will have a place of refuge.
PROVERBS 14:26 NKJV

. . .

We have confidence to enter the
holy place by the blood of Jesus.
HEBREWS 10:19 NASB

. . .

And now, dear children, continue to live in fellowship
with Christ so that when he returns, you will be full
of courage and not shrink back from him in shame.
1 JOHN 2:28 NLT

. . .

We have boldness and access with
confidence through faith in Him.
EPHESIANS 3:12 NKJV

. . .

For the LORD will be your confidence and
will keep your foot from being caught.
PROVERBS 3:26 NASB

And thou, son of man, be not afraid of them,
neither be afraid of their words, though briers and
thorns be with thee, and thou dost dwell among
scorpions: be not afraid of their words, nor be dismayed
at their looks, though they be a rebellious house.
EZEKIEL 2:6 KJV

• • •

Therefore let us draw near with confidence to
the throne of grace, so that we may receive
mercy and find grace to help in time of need.
HEBREWS 4:16 NASB

• • •

Dear friends, if our hearts do not condemn us,
we have confidence before God.
1 JOHN 3:21 NIV

• • •

The wicked flee when no one pursues,
but the righteous are bold as a lion.
PROVERBS 28:1 NKJV

Be brave, be strong.
1 CORINTHIANS 16:13 NKJV

. . .

Be strong and let your heart take courage,
all you who hope in the LORD.
PSALM 31:24 NASB

. . .

By standing firm, you will win your souls.
LUKE 21:19 NLT

. . .

I can do all things through Christ who strengthens me.
PHILIPPIANS 4:13 NKJV

Courage is contagious.
When a brave man takes a stand,
the spines of others are often stiffened.
BILLY GRAHAM

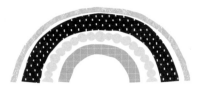

DISCIPLINE

"This is going to hurt me more than it hurts you," is an old line fathers used before spanking their children. Kids have joked about it for years, but it's true—punishment is no fun for anyone involved. It's still vital, though.

Like human fathers, God must correct His children when they disobey Him—and it's all because of His profound love. He truly cares enough to discipline us when we stray from Him. Nobody likes to be punished, but when we learn from our errors, we come closer to God.

Thus you are to know in your heart that the LORD your God was disciplining you just as a man disciplines his son.
DEUTERONOMY 8:5 NASB

. . .

But when we are judged, we are chastened of the Lord, that we should not be condemned with the world.
1 CORINTHIANS 11:32 KJV

. . .

He who keeps instruction is in the way of life, but he who refuses correction goes astray.
PROVERBS 10:17 NKJV

. . .

"Behold, how happy is the man whom God reproves, so do not despise the discipline of the Almighty. For He inflicts pain, and gives relief; He wounds, and His hands also heal."
JOB 5:17–18 NASB

. . .

The fear of the LORD is the beginning of knowledge, but fools despise wisdom and instruction.
PROVERBS 1:7 NKJV

. . .

He who chastens the nations, will He not rebuke, even He who teaches man knowledge?
PSALM 94:10 NASB

And you have forgotten that word of encouragement that addresses you as sons: "My son, do not make light of the Lord's discipline, and do not lose heart when he rebukes you, because the Lord disciplines those he loves, and he punishes everyone he accepts as a son." Endure hardship as discipline; God is treating you as sons. For what son is not disciplined by his father? If you are not disciplined (and everyone undergoes discipline), then you are illegitimate children and not true sons. Moreover, we have all had human fathers who disciplined us and we respected them for it. How much more should we submit to the Father of our spirits and live! Our fathers disciplined us for a little while as they thought best; but God disciplines us for our good, that we may share in his holiness. No discipline seems pleasant at the time, but painful. Later on, however, it produces a harvest of righteousness and peace for those who have been trained by it.

HEBREWS 12:5–11 NIV

• • •

For these commands and this teaching
are a lamp to light the way ahead of you.
The correction of discipline is the way to life.

PROVERBS 6:23 NLT

As many as I love, I rebuke and chasten.
Therefore be zealous and repent.
REVELATION 3:19 NKJV

. . .

Blessed is the man whom You chasten, O LORD,
and whom You teach out of Your law; that You
may grant him relief from the days of adversity,
until a pit is dug for the wicked.
PSALM 94:12–13 NASB

. . .

For whom the LORD loveth he correcteth;
even as a father the son in whom he delighteth.
PROVERBS 3:12 KJV

God has to punish His children from time to time
and it is the very demonstration of His love.
ELISABETH ELLIOT

ENCOURAGEMENT

Want to really be somebody? Don't dream about athletic achievements, or business success, or political power. Be an encourager—you'll have a far more lasting impact on the world around you.

Encouragement comes in many forms: a smile, a phone call, a note, the gift of your time. Make these uplifting acts a habit, and you can change the world—at least your little part of it. Even though you may never know all the effects of your encouragement, be assured that others will remember you as somebody special.

Pure and undefiled religion before God and the Father
is this: to visit orphans and widows in their trouble,
and to keep oneself unspotted from the world.
JAMES 1:27 NKJV

. . .

Therefore encourage one another and build
up one another, just as you also are doing.
1 THESSALONIANS 5:11 NASB

. . .

If we are distressed, it is for your comfort and salvation;
if we are comforted, it is for your comfort,
which produces in you patient endurance
of the same sufferings we suffer.
2 CORINTHIANS 1:6 NIV

. . .

The light of the eyes rejoices the heart,
and a good report makes the bones healthy.
PROVERBS 15:30 NKJV

. . .

So then, brethren, stand firm and hold to the traditions
which you were taught, whether by word of mouth or by
letter from us. Now may our Lord Jesus Christ Himself and
God our Father, who has loved us and given us eternal
comfort and good hope by grace, comfort and strengthen
your hearts in every good work and word.
2 THESSALONIANS 2:15–17 NASB

Don't think only about your own affairs, but be
interested in others, too, and what they are doing.
PHILIPPIANS 2:4 NLT

• • •

He gives power to the weak, and to those
who have no might He increases strength.
ISAIAH 40:29 NKJV

• • •

Little children, let us not love with word
or with tongue, but in deed and truth.
1 JOHN 3:18 NASB

The finest gift you can give anyone is encouragement.
Yet, almost no one gets the encouragement they need to grow to
their full potential. If everyone received the encouragement they
need to grow, the genius in most everyone would blossom and the
world would produce abundance beyond our wildest dreams.
SIDNEY MADWED

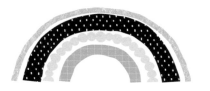

ETERNAL LIFE

You're young, and life seems long. But soon you'll realize that you've been out of school for five, ten, twenty years . . .and you'll know what the Bible means when it says life is "a mist that appears for a little while and then vanishes" (James 4:14 NIV). We can all be thankful that's not the end of the story—God has promised eternal life to those who give their earthly lives to Him. That's a great trade! Live this life in gratitude for God's love for you.

"Most assuredly, I say to you, he who
believes in Me has everlasting life."
JOHN 6:47 NKJV

. . .

"Do not work for the food which perishes, but for the food
which endures to eternal life, which the Son of Man will
give to you, for on Him the Father, God, has set His seal."
JOHN 6:27 NASB

. . .

"And everyone who has left houses or brothers or
sisters or father or mother or children or fields
for my sake will receive a hundred times as
much and will inherit eternal life."
MATTHEW 19:29 NIV

. . .

And when the Chief Shepherd appears, you will
receive the crown of glory that does not fade away.
1 PETER 5:4 NKJV

. . .

The world is passing away, and also its lusts;
but the one who does the will of God lives forever.
1 JOHN 2:17 NASB

. . .

The Spirit of God, who raised Jesus from
the dead, lives in you. And just as he raised
Christ from the dead, he will give life to your
mortal body by this same Spirit living within you.
ROMANS 8:11 NLT

"Most assuredly, I say to you, he who hears
My word and believes in Him who sent Me has
everlasting life, and shall not come into judgment,
but has passed from death into life."
JOHN 5:24 NKJV

. . .

For the one who sows to his own flesh will from the
flesh reap corruption, but the one who sows to the
Spirit will from the Spirit reap eternal life.
GALATIANS 6:8 NASB

. . .

That being justified by his grace, we should be
made heirs according to the hope of eternal life.
TITUS 3:7 KJV

. . .

"For this reason, they are before the throne of God;
and they serve Him day and night in His temple; and He
who sits on the throne will spread His tabernacle over
them. They will hunger no longer, nor thirst anymore;
nor will the sun beat down on them, nor any heat; for the
Lamb in the center of the throne will be their shepherd,
and will guide them to springs of the water of life;
and God will wipe every tear from their eyes."
REVELATION 7:15–17 NASB

We know also that the Son of God has come and has given us understanding, so that we may know him who is true. And we are in him who is true—even in his Son Jesus Christ. He is the true God and eternal life.

1 JOHN 5:20 NIV

. . .

He will give eternal life to those who persist in doing what is good, seeking after the glory and honor and immortality that God offers.

ROMANS 2:7 NLT

. . .

Keep yourselves in God's love as you wait for the mercy of our Lord Jesus Christ to bring you to eternal life.

JUDE 21 NIV

. . .

Blessed be the God and Father of our Lord Jesus Christ, who according to His great mercy has caused us to be born again to a living hope through the resurrection of Jesus Christ from the dead, to obtain an inheritance which is imperishable and undefiled and will not fade away, reserved in heaven for you, who are protected by the power of God through faith for a salvation ready to be revealed in the last time.

1 PETER 1:3–5 NASB

For we know that if our earthly house, this tent,
is destroyed, we have a building from God, a house
not made with hands, eternal in the heavens.
2 CORINTHIANS 5:1 NKJV

. . .

"He who loves his life loses it, and he who hates
his life in this world will keep it to life eternal."
JOHN 12:25 NASB

. . .

For God so loved the world, that he gave his only
begotten Son, that whosoever believeth in him
should not perish, but have everlasting life.
JOHN 3:16 KJV

. . .

Behold, I tell you a mystery: We shall not all sleep, but
we shall all be changed—in a moment, in the twinkling of
an eye, at the last trumpet. For the trumpet will sound,
and the dead will be raised incorruptible, and we shall be
changed. For this corruptible must put on incorruption,
and this mortal must put on immortality. So when this
corruptible has put on incorruption, and this mortal has
put on immortality, then shall be brought to pass the
saying that is written: "Death is swallowed up in victory."
1 CORINTHIANS 15:51–54 NKJV

"And this is eternal life, that they may know You, the only true God, and Jesus Christ whom You have sent."
JOHN 17:3 NKJV

. . .

Jesus said to her, "I am the resurrection and the life; he who believes in Me will live even if he dies, and everyone who lives and believes in Me will never die. Do you believe this?"
JOHN 11:25–26 NASB

. . .

But now that you have been set free from sin and have become slaves to God, the benefit you reap leads to holiness, and the result is eternal life. For the wages of sin is death, but the gift of God is eternal life in Christ Jesus our Lord.
ROMANS 6:22–23 NIV

. . .

And this is the testimony: that God has given us eternal life, and this life is in His Son. He who has the Son has life; he who does not have the Son of God does not have life. These things I have written to you who believe in the name of the Son of God, that you may know that you have eternal life, and that you may continue to believe in the name of the Son of God.
1 JOHN 5:11–13 NKJV

Many of those who sleep in the dust of the ground will awake, these to everlasting life, but the others to disgrace and everlasting contempt.
DANIEL 12:2 NASB

. . .

This truth gives them the confidence of eternal life, which God promised them before the world began—and he cannot lie.
TITUS 1:2 NLT

. . .

Fight the good fight of faith; take hold of the eternal life to which you were called, and you made the good confession in the presence of many witnesses.
1 TIMOTHY 6:12 NASB

. . .

Let that therefore abide in you, which ye have heard from the beginning. If that which ye have heard from the beginning shall remain in you, ye also shall continue in the Son, and in the Father. And this is the promise that he hath promised us, even eternal life.
1 JOHN 2:24–25 KJV

. . .

"And I give them eternal life, and they shall never perish; neither shall anyone snatch them out of My hand."
JOHN 10:28 NKJV

In the future there is laid up for me the crown of righteousness, which the Lord, the righteous Judge, will award to me on that day; and not only to me, but also to all who have loved His appearing.

2 TIMOTHY 4:8 NASB

. . .

"In my Father's house are many rooms; if it were not so, I would have told you. I am going there to prepare a place for you. And if I go and prepare a place for you, I will come back and take you to be with me that you also may be where I am."

JOHN 14:2–3 NIV

. . .

There shall be no night there: They need no lamp nor light of the sun, for the Lord God gives them light. And they shall reign forever and ever.

REVELATION 22:5 NKJV

When you were born, you cried and everybody else was happy. The only question that matters is this: When you die, will you be happy when everybody else is crying?

TONY CAMPOLO

FAITH

"Ya gotta have faith," many say. The question is, faith in what? Make sure you put your faith into something (actually, *Someone*) worthy. In a word, God.

Of course, in a world of uncertainty, faith sometimes seems out of reach. But remember this: God exists, and He never changes. We can put our complete faith in Him, and He will never fail us.

For we walk by faith, not by sight.
2 CORINTHIANS 5:7 NKJV

. . .

In addition to all, taking up the shield of faith
with which you will be able to extinguish
all the flaming arrows of the evil one.
EPHESIANS 6:16 NASB

. . .

Listen, my dear brothers: Has not God chosen those who
are poor in the eyes of the world to be rich in faith and to
inherit the kingdom he promised those who love him?
JAMES 2:5 NIV

. . .

Now the purpose of the commandment is love from a pure
heart, from a good conscience, and from sincere faith.
1 TIMOTHY 1:5 NKJV

. . .

And He said to the woman, "Your faith
has saved you; go in peace."
LUKE 7:50 NASB

. . .

For when your faith is tested, your endurance
has a chance to grow. So let it grow, for when
your endurance is fully developed, you will be
strong in character and ready for anything.
JAMES 1:3-4 NLT

Trust in the LORD with all your heart,
and lean not on your own understanding.
PROVERBS 3:5 NKJV

. . .

"For I will certainly rescue you, and you will not fall by
the sword; but you will have your own life as booty,
because you have trusted in Me," declares the LORD.
JEREMIAH 39:18 NASB

. . .

Now faith is the substance of things hoped for,
the evidence of things not seen.
HEBREWS 11:1 KJV

. . .

And my speech and my preaching were not with
persuasive words of human wisdom, but in demonstration
of the Spirit and of power, that your faith should not be in
the wisdom of men but in the power of God.
1 CORINTHIANS 2:4–5 NKJV

. . .

But as many as received Him, to them He
gave the right to become children of God,
even to those who believe in His name.
JOHN 1:12 NASB

. . .

Thou wilt keep him in perfect peace, whose mind
is stayed on thee: because he trusteth in thee.
ISAIAH 26:3 KJV

I myself no longer live, but Christ lives in me. So I
live my life in this earthly body by trusting in the
Son of God, who loved me and gave himself for me.
GALATIANS 2:20 NLT

. . .

This charge I commit to you, son Timothy,
according to the prophecies previously made
concerning you, that by them you may wage the
good warfare, having faith and a good conscience.
1 TIMOTHY 1:18–19 NKJV

. . .

For in it the righteousness of God is revealed
from faith to faith; as it is written, "But the
righteous man shall live by faith."
ROMANS 1:17 NASB

. . .

So the Lord said, "If you have faith as a mustard seed,
you can say to this mulberry tree, 'Be pulled up by the
roots and be planted in the sea,' and it would obey you."
LUKE 17:6 NKJV

. . .

Blessed is the man who trusts in the LORD and whose trust
is the LORD. For he will be like a tree planted by the water,
that extends its roots by a stream and will not fear when
the heat comes; but its leaves will be green, and it will not
be anxious in a year of drought nor cease to yield fruit.
JEREMIAH 17:7–8 NASB

For you are all sons of God through faith in Christ Jesus.
GALATIANS 3:26 NKJV

. . .

Is any one of you sick? He should call the elders
of the church to pray over him and anoint him with
oil in the name of the Lord. And the prayer offered
in faith will make the sick person well; the Lord will
raise him up. If he has sinned, he will be forgiven.
JAMES 5:14–15 NIV

. . .

So then faith comes by hearing,
and hearing by the word of God.
ROMANS 10:17 NKJV

. . .

And without faith it is impossible to please Him,
for he who comes to God must believe that He is
and that He is a rewarder of those who seek Him.
HEBREWS 11:6 NASB

. . .

"Everything is possible for him who believes."
MARK 9:23 NIV

. . .

Though you have not seen Him, you love Him, and though
you do not see Him now, but believe in Him, you greatly
rejoice with joy inexpressible and full of glory.
1 PETER 1:8 NASB

Jesus saith unto him, Thomas, because thou hast
seen me, thou hast believed: blessed are they
that have not seen, and yet have believed.
JOHN 20:29 KJV

. . .

Let us go right into the presence of God, with true
hearts fully trusting him. For our evil consciences have
been sprinkled with Christ's blood to make us clean,
and our bodies have been washed with pure water.
HEBREWS 10:22 NLT

. . .

But if any of you lacks wisdom, let him ask of God,
who gives to all generously and without reproach,
and it will be given to him. But he must ask in faith
without any doubting, for the one who doubts is like
the surf of the sea, driven and tossed by the wind.
JAMES 1:5–6 NASB

Faith means believing that Jesus is who He says He is
(God), that He did what He said He did (died for our sins),
and that He will do for us what He said He would do
(forgive our sins and give us eternal life).
PATRICK MORLEY

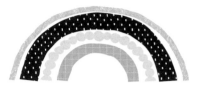

FINANCES

Surveys often show that "making money" is a top priority of graduating college seniors. Sure, we all need money to live on. . .but should a fat bank account be our primary goal?

Money is a source of both joy and trial in our lives. In the proper perspective, money can be a useful, helpful thing. The wrong emphasis, however, can lead to grief—and possibly sin. God has a lot to say about money in the Bible. Learn His priorities, and honor Him with your finances.

A good name is to be chosen rather than great riches,
loving favor rather than silver and gold. . . . By humility
and the fear of the Lord are riches and honor and life.
PROVERBS 22:1, 4 NKJV

. . . .

Make sure that your character is free from the
love of money, being content with what you have;
for He Himself has said, "I will never desert you,
nor will I ever forsake you."
HEBREWS 13:5 NASB

. . . .

Do not withhold good from those who deserve it
when it's in your power to help them. If you can
help your neighbor now, don't say, "Come back
tomorrow, and then I'll help you."
PROVERBS 3:27–28 NLT

. . . .

"Give, and it will be given to you: good measure,
pressed down, shaken together, and running over will
be put into your bosom. For with the same measure
that you use, it will be measured back to you."
LUKE 6:38 NKJV

. . . .

In this case, moreover, it is required of
stewards that one be found trustworthy.
1 CORINTHIANS 4:2 NASB

And it is a good thing to receive wealth from God and the good health to enjoy it. To enjoy your work and accept your lot in life—that is indeed a gift from God.
ECCLESIASTES 5:19 NLT

• • •

But those who want to get rich fall into temptation and a snare and many foolish and harmful desires which plunge men into ruin and destruction. For the love of money is a root of all sorts of evil, and some by longing for it have wandered away from the faith and pierced themselves with many griefs. But flee from these things, you man of God, and pursue righteousness, godliness, faith, love, perseverance and gentleness.
1 TIMOTHY 6:9–11 NASB

• • •

The rich ruleth over the poor, and the borrower is servant to the lender.
PROVERBS 22:7 KJV

• • •

And He said to them, "Render therefore to Caesar the things that are Caesar's, and to God the things that are God's."
MATTHEW 22:21 NKJV

• • •

"Every man shall give as he is able, according to the blessing of the LORD your God which He has given you."
DEUTERONOMY 16:17 NASB

"I tell you, use worldly wealth to gain friends for yourselves, so that when it is gone, you will be welcomed into eternal dwellings. Whoever can be trusted with very little can also be trusted with much, and whoever is dishonest with very little will also be dishonest with much. So if you have not been trustworthy in handling worldly wealth, who will trust you with true riches? And if you have not been trustworthy with someone else's property, who will give you property of your own?"
LUKE 16:9–12 NIV

. . .

Riches do not profit in the day of wrath,
but righteousness delivers from death.
PROVERBS 11:4 NKJV

. . .

"No one can serve two masters; for either he will hate the one and love the other, or else he will be loyal to the one and despise the other. You cannot serve God and mammon."
MATTHEW 6:24 NKJV

. . .

Do not be among those who give pledges,
among those who become guarantors for
debts. If you have nothing with which to pay,
why should he take your bed from under you?
PROVERBS 22:26–27 NASB

Lord, who shall abide in thy tabernacle? who shall dwell in thy holy hill? . . . He that putteth not out his money to usury, nor taketh reward against the innocent. He that doeth these things shall never be moved.
PSALM 15:1, 5 KJV

. . .

"For which of you, intending to build a tower, does not sit down first and count the cost, whether he has enough to finish it—lest, after he has laid the foundation, and is not able to finish, all who see it begin to mock him, saying, 'This man began to build and was not able to finish'?"
LUKE 14:28–30 NKJV

. . .

He who trusts in his riches will fall, but the righteous will flourish like the green leaf.
PROVERBS 11:28 NASB

. . .

"So when you give to the needy, do not announce it with trumpets, as the hypocrites do in the synagogues and on the streets, to be honored by men. I tell you the truth, they have received their reward in full. But when you give to the needy, do not let your left hand know what your right hand is doing, so that your giving may be in secret. Then your Father, who sees what is done in secret, will reward you."
MATTHEW 6:2–4 NIV

I have shown you in every way, by laboring like this, that you must support the weak. And remember the words of the Lord Jesus, that He said, "It is more blessed to give than to receive."

ACTS 20:35 NKJV

. . .

There is a grievous evil which I have seen under the sun: riches being hoarded by their owner to his hurt. When those riches were lost through a bad investment and he had fathered a son, then there was nothing to support him. As he had come naked from his mother's womb, so will he return as he came. He will take nothing from the fruit of his labor that he can carry in his hand.

ECCLESIASTES 5:13–15 NASB

. . .

Some who are poor pretend to be rich;
others who are rich pretend to be poor.

PROVERBS 13:7 NLT

. . .

Command those who are rich in this present age not to be haughty, nor to trust in uncertain riches but in the living God, who gives us richly all things to enjoy.

1 TIMOTHY 6:17–19 NKJV

. . .

One who is gracious to a poor man lends to the LORD, and He will repay him for his good deed.

PROVERBS 19:17 NASB

And He said to them, "Take heed and beware of covetousness, for one's life does not consist in the abundance of the things he possesses."
LUKE 12:15 NKJV

. . .

Honour the LORD with thy substance, and with the firstfruits of all thine increase: So shall thy barns be filled with plenty, and thy presses shall burst out with new wine.
PROVERBS 3:9–10 KJV

. . .

"But you shall remember the LORD your God, for it is He who is giving you power to make wealth, that He may confirm His covenant which He swore to your fathers, as it is this day."
DEUTERONOMY 8:18 NASB

. . .

Each man should give what he has decided in his heart to give, not reluctantly or under compulsion, for God loves a cheerful giver.
2 CORINTHIANS 9:7 NIV

. . .

Let the lowly brother glory in his exaltation, but the rich in his humiliation, because as a flower of the field he will pass away. For no sooner has the sun risen with a burning heat than it withers the grass; its flower falls, and its beautiful appearance perishes. So the rich man also will fade away in his pursuits.
JAMES 1:9–11 NKJV

"And others are the ones on whom seed was sown among the thorns; these are the ones who have heard the word, but the worries of the world, and the deceitfulness of riches, and the desires for other things enter in and choke the word, and it becomes unfruitful."
MARK 4:18–19 NASB

. . .

After all, we didn't bring anything with us when we came into the world, and we certainly cannot carry anything with us when we die. So if we have enough food and clothing, let us be content.
1 TIMOTHY 6:7–8 NLT

. . .

Wealth obtained by fraud dwindles,
but the one who gathers by labor increases it.
PROVERBS 13:11 NASB

. . .

Give freely without begrudging it, and the LORD your God will bless you in everything you do.
DEUTERONOMY 15:10 NLT

. . .

Do not trust in oppression and do not vainly hope in robbery; if riches increase, do not set your heart upon them.
PSALM 62:10 NASB

"Therefore I say to you, do not worry about your life, what you will eat or what you will drink; nor about your body, what you will put on. Is not life more than food and the body more than clothing? Look at the birds of the air, for they neither sow nor reap nor gather into barns; yet your heavenly Father feeds them. Are you not of more value than they? Which of you by worrying can add one cubit to his stature? So why do you worry about clothing? Consider the lilies of the field, how they grow: they neither toil nor spin; and yet I say to you that even Solomon in all his glory was not arrayed like one of these. Now if God so clothes the grass of the field, which today is, and tomorrow is thrown into the oven, will He not much more clothe you, O you of little faith? Therefore do not worry, saying, 'What shall we eat?' or 'What shall we drink?' or 'What shall we wear?' For after all these things the Gentiles seek. For your heavenly Father knows that you need all these things. But seek first the kingdom of God and His righteousness, and all these things shall be added to you."

MATTHEW 6:25–33 NKJV

• • •

If then you were raised with Christ, seek those things which are above, where Christ is, sitting at the right hand of God. Set your mind on things above, not on things on the earth.

COLOSSIANS 3:1–2 NKJV

Lay not up for yourselves treasures upon earth, where moth and rust doth corrupt, and where thieves break through and steal: But lay up for yourselves treasures in heaven, where neither moth nor rust doth corrupt, and where thieves do not break through nor steal: For where your treasure is, there will your heart be also.
MATTHEW 6:19–21 KJV

[We should] spend no more than we make on a monthly basis. Ideally that means to live on a cash basis and not use credit or borrowed money to provide normal living expenses. It also means the self-discipline to control spending and keep needs, wants, and desires in their proper relationship.
LARRY BURKETT

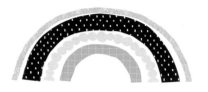

FORGIVENESS

How many times have you heard someone say, "I could never forgive him for (list offense here)"? Forgiving others is not easy to do, especially if the other person hasn't asked for forgiveness. But God's Word is clear: We are to forgive others just as He has forgiven us. Wow—too hard, you say? Sure it is, humanly speaking. But God also gives us the ability through His Spirit. Be sure to confess your sins to Him and ask Him to forgive you. Then ask forgiveness of others whom you may have offended. Being faithful in these areas will make it easier for you to forgive others.

"Do not judge, and you will not be judged.
Do not condemn, and you will not be condemned.
Forgive, and you will be forgiven."
LUKE 6:37 NIV

. . .

The discretion of a man makes him slow to anger,
and his glory is to overlook a transgression.
PROVERBS 19:11 NKJV

. . .

"But I say to you, do not resist an evil person;
but whoever slaps you on your right cheek, turn the
other to him also. If anyone wants to sue you and
take your shirt, let him have your coat also. Whoever
forces you to go one mile, go with him two."
MATTHEW 5:39–41 NASB

. . .

None of their past sins will be brought up again, for they
have done what is just and right, and they will surely live.
EZEKIEL 33:16 NLT

. . .

And be ye kind one to another, tenderhearted,
forgiving one another, even as God for
Christ's sake hath forgiven you.
EPHESIANS 4:32 KJV

Bless the LORD, O my soul, and forget none of
His benefits; Who pardons all your iniquities,
Who heals all your diseases.
PSALM 103:2–3 NASB

. . .

"And forgive us our sins, for we also
forgive everyone who is indebted to us."
LUKE 11:4 NKJV

. . .

"No more shall every man teach his neighbor,
and every man his brother, saying, 'Know the LORD,'
for they all shall know Me, from the least of them to the
greatest of them, says the LORD. For I will forgive their
iniquity, and their sin I will remember no more."
JEREMIAH 31:34 NKJV

. . .

If we confess our sins, He is faithful and
righteous to forgive us our sins and to
cleanse us from all unrighteousness.
1 JOHN 1:9 NASB

. . .

Then Peter came to Jesus and asked, "Lord,
how many times shall I forgive my brother when he
sins against me? Up to seven times?" Jesus answered,
"I tell you, not seven times, but seventy-seven times."
MATTHEW 18:21–22 NIV

Who is a God like You, pardoning iniquity and passing over the transgression of the remnant of His heritage? He does not retain His anger forever, because He delights in mercy.
MICAH 7:18 NKJV

. . .

Be gracious to me, O God, according to Your lovingkindness; according to the greatness of Your compassion blot out my transgressions.
PSALM 51:1 NASB

. . .

"But when you are praying, first forgive anyone you are holding a grudge against, so that your Father in heaven will forgive your sins, too."
MARK 11:25 NLT

. . .

For this is My blood of the new covenant, which is shed for many for the remission of sins.
MATTHEW 26:28 NKJV

. . .

. . .not returning evil for evil or insult for insult, but giving a blessing instead; for you were called for the very purpose that you might inherit a blessing.
1 PETER 3:9 NASB

"For if you forgive men their trespasses,
your heavenly Father will also forgive you.
But if you do not forgive men their trespasses,
neither will your Father forgive your trespasses."
MATTHEW 6:14–15 NKJV

· · ·

Therefore, as the elect of God, holy and beloved,
put on tender mercies, kindness, humility, meekness,
longsuffering; bearing with one another, and forgiving
one another, if anyone has a complaint against another;
even as Christ forgave you, so you also must do.
COLOSSIANS 3:12–13 NKJV

· · ·

How blessed is he whose transgression
is forgiven, whose sin is covered!
PSALM 32:1 NASB

· · ·

"For I will forgive their wickedness
and will remember their sins no more."
HEBREWS 8:12 NIV

Forgiveness is the oil of relationships.
JOSH MCDOWELL

GOD'S LOVE

Everybody talks about love. But most of the "love" they're discussing falls far short of the real thing: God's love for His children. God loves with a love beyond human comprehension. He knows everything about you—your needs, your desires, and your dreams—and wants the best for you. That's why He sent His only Son, Jesus, to die on a cross for your sins. Through good times and bad, God will always be with you, loving you more than you could ever imagine.

For it is You who blesses the righteous man, O LORD,
You surround him with favor as with a shield.
PSALM 5:12 NASB

. . .

"For God so loved the world that he gave his
only Son, so that everyone who believes in
him will not perish but have eternal life."
JOHN 3:16 NLT

. . .

"Are not five sparrows sold for two copper coins?
And not one of them is forgotten before God. But the
very hairs of your head are all numbered. Do not fear
therefore; you are of more value than many sparrows."
LUKE 12:6–7 NKJV

. . .

And we know that God causes all things to
work together for good to those who love God,
to those who are called according to His purpose.
ROMANS 8:28 NASB

. . .

Those who know your name trust in you, for you, O LORD,
have never abandoned anyone who searches for you.
PSALM 9:10 NLT

. . .

"Lo, I am with you always, even to the end of the age."
MATTHEW 28:20 NASB

"I will heal their backsliding, I will love them freely,
for My anger has turned away from him."
HOSEA 14:4 NKJV

. . .

He will fulfil the desire of them that fear him: he also will
hear their cry, and will save them. The LORD preserveth all
them that love him: but all the wicked will he destroy.
PSALM 145:19–20 KJV

. . .

Now hope does not disappoint, because the
love of God has been poured out in our hearts
by the Holy Spirit who was given to us.
ROMANS 5:5 NKJV

. . .

"For the LORD your God is a compassionate God;
He will not fail you nor destroy you nor forget the
covenant with your fathers which He swore to them."
DEUTERONOMY 4:31 NASB

. . .

"I knew that you are a gracious and compassionate God,
slow to anger and abounding in love, a God
who relents from sending calamity."
JONAH 4:2 NIV

But You, O Lord, are a God merciful and gracious,
slow to anger and abundant in loving kindness and truth.
PSALM 86:15 NASB

. . .

For the Father himself loveth you, because ye have
loved me, and have believed that I came out from God.
JOHN 16:27 KJV

. . .

For I am persuaded that neither death nor life,
nor angels nor principalities nor powers, nor things
present nor things to come, nor height nor depth,
nor any other created thing, shall be able to separate us
from the love of God which is in Christ Jesus our Lord.
ROMANS 8:38–39 NKJV

. . .

As for God, His way is blameless; the word of the LORD is
tried; He is a shield to all who take refuge in Him.
PSALM 18:30 NASB

. . .

God showed how much he loved us by sending
his only Son into the world so that we might have
eternal life through him. This is real love. It is not
that we loved God, but that he loved us and sent
his Son as a sacrifice to take away our sins.
1 JOHN 4:9–10 NLT

And we have known and believed the love that
God has for us. God is love, and he who abides
in love abides in God, and God in him.
1 JOHN 4:16 NKJV

. . . .

But the LORD is with me as a mighty,
awesome One. Therefore my persecutors
will stumble, and will not prevail. They will be
greatly ashamed, for they will not prosper.
Their everlasting confusion will never be forgotten.
JEREMIAH 20:11 NKJV

. . . .

The LORD will guard your going out and your
coming in from this time forth and forever.
PSALM 121:8 NASB

. . . .

And my God will meet all your needs according
to his glorious riches in Christ Jesus.
PHILIPPIANS 4:19 NIV

. . . .

Every good gift and every perfect gift is from above,
and comes down from the Father of lights, with whom
there is no variation or shadow of turning. Of His own
will He brought us forth by the word of truth, that we
might be a kind of firstfruits of His creatures.
JAMES 1:17–18 NKJV

Many are the sorrows of the wicked, but he who trusts
in the LORD, lovingkindness shall surround him.
PSALM 32:10 NASB

. . .

But God showed his great love for us by sending
Christ to die for us while we were still sinners.
ROMANS 5:8 NLT

. . .

Behold what manner of love the Father has bestowed
on us, that we should be called children of God!
1 JOHN 3:1 NKJV

In God, we have a Father who thinks of us unceasingly.
We are never absent from His thoughts. . .and this is a
Father who not only desires to see good in my life, He has
the will and power and wisdom to cause it to happen!
JAMES ROBISON

GOD'S PROVISION

"But, Mom, I really need that new sweater. . . ."

"But, Dad, I really need that car. . . ."

One of the most important lessons in life is learning to distinguish between needs and wants. For Christians, the needs are taken care of: God has promised to meet all of them. The wants, of course, are another matter, but as we grow closer to God, they'll likely become less and less of an issue. He knows what is best for us—just trust that He'll take care of you as He has promised.

The young lions do lack and suffer hunger;
but they who seek the LORD shall not
be in want of any good thing.
PSALM 34:10 NASB

. . .

"For this reason I say to you, do not be worried about your life, as to what you will eat or what you will drink; nor for your body, as to what you will put on. Is not life more than food, and the body more than clothing? Look at the birds of the air, that they do not sow, nor reap nor gather into barns, and yet your heavenly Father feeds them. Are you not worth much more than they? And who of you by being worried can add a single hour to his life? And why are you worried about clothing? Observe how the lilies of the field grow; they do not toil nor do they spin, yet I say to you that not even Solomon in all his glory clothed himself like one of these. "But if God so clothes the grass of the field, which is alive today and tomorrow is thrown into the furnace, will He not much more clothe you? You of little faith! Do not worry then, saying, 'What will we eat?' or 'What will we drink?' or 'What will we wear for clothing?' For the Gentiles eagerly seek all these things; for your heavenly Father knows that you need all these things. But seek first His kingdom and His righteousness, and all these things will be added to you."
MATTHEW 6:25–33 NASB

He has given food to those who fear Him;
He will ever be mindful of His covenant.
PSALM 111:5 NKJV

• • •

But my God shall supply all your need according
to his riches in glory by Christ Jesus.
PHILIPPIANS 4:19 KJV

• • •

Command those who are rich in this present world not
to be arrogant nor to put their hope in wealth, which is
so uncertain, but to put their hope in God, who richly
provides us with everything for our enjoyment.
1 TIMOTHY 6:17 NIV

Lift up your eyes. Your heavenly Father waits
to bless you in inconceivable ways to make your
life what you never dreamed it could be.
ANNE ORTLUND

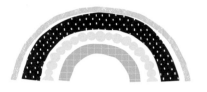

GRATITUDE

Thanksgiving—a day in November, right? Well, not entirely. Thanksgiving should be a continuous attitude expressed by the Christian. We all have many reasons to thank God—take a few minutes to list His blessings, and you'll be amazed at what He's done for you. Give God praise for what He has done in your life—and for what He will do in the future.

I will praise the name of God with a song, and will magnify
Him with thanksgiving. This also shall please the LORD
better than an ox or bull, which has horns and hooves.
PSALM 69:30–31 NKJV

. . .

Is anyone among you suffering? Then he must pray.
Is anyone cheerful? He is to sing praises.
JAMES 5:13 NASB

. . .

Then you will sing psalms and hymns and spiritual songs
among yourselves, making music to the Lord in your
hearts. And you will always give thanks for everything to
God the Father in the name of our Lord Jesus Christ.
EPHESIANS 5:19–20 NLT

. . .

Oh come, let us sing to the LORD! let us shout
joyfully to the Rock of our salvation. Let us
come before His presence with thanksgiving;
let us shout joyfully to Him with psalms.
PSALM 95:1–2 NKJV

. . .

In everything give thanks; for this is
God's will for you in Christ Jesus.
1 THESSALONIANS 5:18 NASB

But thanks be to God, which giveth us the
victory through our Lord Jesus Christ.
1 CORINTHIANS 15:57 KJV

. . .

I will wash my hands in innocence; so I will go about
Your altar, O LORD, that I may proclaim with the voice
of thanksgiving, and tell of all Your wondrous works.
PSALM 26:6–7 NKJV

. . .

O give thanks to the LORD, for He is good;
for His lovingkindness is everlasting.
1 CHRONICLES 16:34 NASB

. . .

For every creature of God is good, and nothing
to be refused, if it be received with thanksgiving.
1 TIMOTHY 4:4 KJV

. . .

It is good to give thanks to the LORD, and to sing praises
to Your name, O Most High; to declare Your lovingkindness
in the morning, and Your faithfulness every night.
PSALM 92:1–2 NKJV

. . .

He took the seven loaves and the fish; and giving thanks,
He broke them and started giving them to the disciples,
and the disciples gave them to the people.
MATTHEW 15:36 NASB

And whatever you do or say, let it be as a
representative of the Lord Jesus, all the while
giving thanks through him to God the Father.
COLOSSIANS 3:17 NLT

. . .

I will praise You, O LORD, with my whole heart;
I will tell of all Your marvelous works.
PSALM 9:1 NKJV

. . .

And in that day you will say, "Give thanks to the LORD, call
on His name. Make known His deeds among the peoples;
make them remember that His name is exalted."
ISAIAH 12:4 NASB

. . .

Therefore, since we are receiving a kingdom that
cannot be shaken, let us be thankful, and so
worship God acceptably with reverence and awe.
HEBREWS 12:28 NIV

True thanksgiving means that we need to
thank God for what He has done for us,
and not to tell Him what we have done for Him.
GEORGE HENDRICK

HONESTY

Let's be honest—honesty is by no means a popular choice in our world today, nor is it an easy one. Look around, and you'll see examples of dishonesty every day, from politicians, lawyers, bosses. . .and maybe even ourselves (if we're honest about it!). But God expects more of His children. We are commanded to be truthful, as followers of Jesus Christ, who is the Truth. Push yourself to be honest, just like you'd push yourself toward any worthwhile goal, and God will bless you for following the truth.

Lying lips are an abomination to the LORD,
but those who deal faithfully are His delight.
PROVERBS 12:22 NASB

. . .

I will maintain my righteousness and never let go of it;
my conscience will not reproach me as long as I live.
JOB 27:6 NIV

. . .

But we have renounced the hidden things of shame,
not walking in craftiness nor handling the word of God
deceitfully, but by manifestation of the truth commending
ourselves to every man's conscience in the sight of God.
2 CORINTHIANS 4:2 NKJV

. . .

Pray for us, for we are sure that we have
a good conscience, desiring to conduct
ourselves honorably in all things.
HEBREWS 13:18 NASB

. . .

"Do not use dishonest standards when measuring length,
weight, or volume. Your scales and weights must be
accurate. Your containers for measuring dry goods or
liquids must be accurate. I, the LORD, am your God."
LEVITICUS 19:35–36 NLT

Honest weights and scales are the LORD's;
all the weights in the bag are His work.
PROVERBS 16:11 NKJV

. . .

"In everything, therefore, treat people the
same way you want them to treat you,
for this is the Law and the Prophets."
MATTHEW 7:12 NASB

. . .

And herein do I exercise myself, to have always a
conscience void to offence toward God, and toward men.
ACTS 24:16 KJV

. . .

Finally, brethren, whatever is true, whatever is honorable,
whatever is right, whatever is pure, whatever is lovely,
whatever is of good repute, if there is any excellence
and if anything worthy of praise, dwell on these things.
The things you have learned and received and
heard and seen in me, practice these things,
and the God of peace will be with you.
PHILIPPIANS 4:8–9 NASB

. . .

The LORD abhors dishonest scales,
but accurate weights are his delight.
PROVERBS 11:1 NIV

"Do not cheat one another. Do not lie."
LEVITICUS 19:11 NLT

• • •

Do not lie to one another, since you have put
off the old man with his deeds, and have put
on the new man who is renewed in knowledge
according to the image of Him who created him.
COLOSSIANS 3:9–10 NKJV

• • •

"Treat others the same way you
want them to treat you."
LUKE 6:31 NASB

Honesty is the best policy, as the saying goes.
It works in business as it does in all of life. Without
honesty, relationships fail, business turns sour,
and self-respect goes right out the door. Honesty is
the bedrock upon which we build our marriages,
conduct our businesses, and sell our products.
EDWARD HAYES

HUMILITY

Anyone want to be humiliated? I don't see any hands going up.

While humiliation is a negative thing, humility is very positive—something to be desired. Being humble is not a sign of weakness; you could view it as "quiet strength." Think about Jesus—Philippians 2:8 speaks of Christ's humility, followed by His obedience. He died on the cross for us because of His humility. Imagine what great things you could accomplish for God if you followed Jesus' humble example.

But he giveth more grace. Wherefore he saith,
God resisteth the proud, but giveth grace unto
the humble. Submit yourselves therefore to God.
Resist the devil, and he will flee from you.
JAMES 4:6–7 KJV

. . .

By humility and the fear of the
LORD are riches and honor and life.
PROVERBS 22:4 NKJV

. . .

The humble have seen it and are glad;
you who seek God, let your heart revive.
PSALM 69:32 NASB

. . .

Your attitude should be the same as that of
Christ Jesus: Who, being in very nature God, did not
consider equality with God something to be grasped,
but made himself nothing, taking the very nature of
a servant, being made in human likeness. And being
found in appearance as a man, he humbled himself
and became obedient to death—even death on a cross!
Therefore God exalted him to the highest place and gave
him the name that is above every name, that at the name
of Jesus every knee should bow, in heaven and on earth
and under the earth, and every tongue confess that
Jesus Christ is Lord, to the glory of God the Father.
PHILIPPIANS 2:5–11 NIV

When pride cometh, then cometh shame:
but with the lowly is wisdom.
PROVERBS 11:2 KJV

. . .

You younger men, likewise, be subject to your
elders; and all of you, clothe yourselves with humility
toward one another, for "God is opposed to the
proud, but gives grace to the humble." Therefore
humble yourselves under the mighty hand of God,
that He may exalt you at the proper time.
1 PETER 5:5–6 NASB

. . .

"I tell you, this sinner, not the Pharisee, returned
home justified before God. For the proud will be
humbled, but the humble will be honored."
LUKE 18:14 NLT

. . .

For thus says the High and Lofty One who inhabits
eternity, whose name is Holy: "I dwell in the high
and holy place, with him who has a contrite and
humble spirit, to revive the spirit of the humble,
and to revive the heart of the contrite ones."
ISAIAH 57:15 NKJV

. . .

The fear of the LORD is the instruction for wisdom,
and before honor comes humility.
PROVERBS 15:33 NASB

And whosoever shall exalt himself shall be abased;
and he that shall humble himself shall be exalted.
MATTHEW 23:12 KJV

. . .

Therefore if there is any consolation in Christ,
if any comfort of love, if any fellowship of the Spirit,
if any affection and mercy, fulfill my joy by being
like-minded, having the same love, being of one
accord, of one mind. Let nothing be done through
selfish ambition or conceit, but in lowliness of mind
let each esteem others better than himself.
PHILIPPIANS 2:1–3 NKJV

. . .

For though the LORD is exalted, yet He regards
the lowly, but the haughty He knows from afar.
PSALM 138:6 NASB

Do you aspire to great things? Begin with little ones.
You desire to erect a very high building? Think first of
the foundation of humility. The higher you intend it,
the deeper must the foundations be laid.
SAINT AUGUSTINE

JOY

It seems like everyone's looking for happiness these days—from money, possessions, entertainment, you name it. But any pleasure that those things bring is short-lived.

True joy, however, is the deep-down, long-lasting satisfaction of a right relationship with God, the source of all good things. You can experience His gift of joy today, and every day. Just don't keep it to yourself—be sure to spread it to others around you. They're probably looking for some!

Dear brothers and sisters, whenever trouble
comes your way, let it be an opportunity for joy.
JAMES 1:2 NLT

. . .

Now may the God of hope fill you with all joy
and peace in believing, that you may abound
in hope by the power of the Holy Spirit.
ROMANS 15:13 NKJV

. . .

"Truly, truly, I say to you, that you will weep and
lament, but the world will rejoice; you will grieve,
but your grief will be turned into joy."
JOHN 16:20 NASB

. . .

Speaking to yourselves in psalms and hymns
and spiritual songs, singing and making
melody in your heart to the Lord. . .
EPHESIANS 5:19 KJV

. . .

The LORD is my strength and my shield; my heart trusted
in Him, and I am helped; therefore my heart greatly
rejoices, and with my song I will praise Him.
PSALM 28:7 NKJV

Rejoicing in hope, persevering in
tribulation, devoted to prayer. . .
ROMANS 12:12 NASB

. . .

You will go out in joy and be led forth in peace;
the mountains and hills will burst into song before you,
and all the trees of the field will clap their hands.
ISAIAH 55:12 NIV

. . .

My lips shall greatly rejoice when I sing to You,
and my soul, which You have redeemed.
PSALM 71:23 NKJV

. . .

"You have made known to me the ways of life;
you will make me full of gladness with your presence."
ACTS 2:28 NASB

. . .

Those who plant in tears will harvest with shouts
of joy. They weep as they go to plant their seed,
but they sing as they return with the harvest.
PSALM 126:5–6 NLT

. . .

"These things I have spoken to you, that My joy
may remain in you, and that your joy may be full."
JOHN 15:11 NKJV

"He will yet fill your mouth with laughter
and your lips with shouting."
JOB 8:21 NASB

. . .

But let all those that put their trust in thee rejoice:
let them ever shout for joy, because thou defendest them:
let them also that love thy name be joyful in thee.
PSALM 5:11 KJV

. . .

"Then shall the virgin rejoice in the dance,
and the young men and the old, together; for I
will turn their mourning to joy, will comfort them,
and make them rejoice rather than sorrow."
JEREMIAH 31:13 NKJV

. . .

"I will rejoice greatly in the LORD, my soul will exult
in my God; for He has clothed me with garments
of salvation, He has wrapped me with a robe of
righteousness, as a bridegroom decks himself with a
garland, and as a bride adorns herself with her jewels."
ISAIAH 61:10 NASB

. . .

Rejoice in the LORD and be glad, you righteous;
sing, all you who are upright in heart!
PSALM 32:11 NIV

Rejoice in the LORD always. Again I will say, rejoice!
PHILIPPIANS 4:4 NKJV

• • •

"Until now you have asked for nothing in My name; ask and
you will receive, so that your joy may be made full."
JOHN 16:24 NASB

• • •

You will show me the way of life, granting me the joy of
your presence and the pleasures of living with you forever.
PSALM 16:11 NLT

• • •

"Rejoice in that day and leap for joy! For indeed
your reward is great in heaven, for in like
manner their fathers did to the prophets."
LUKE 6:23 NKJV

• • •

"But now I come to You; and these things
I speak in the world so that they may have
My joy made full in themselves."
JOHN 17:13 NASB

• • •

Rejoice evermore. . . . In every thing give thanks:
for this is the will of God in Christ Jesus concerning you.
1 THESSALONIANS 5:16, 18 KJV

So the ransomed of the LORD shall return,
and come to Zion with singing, with everlasting
joy on their heads. They shall obtain joy and gladness;
sorrow and sighing shall flee away.
ISAIAH 51:11 NKJV

· · ·

Shout joyfully to the LORD, all the earth. Serve the LORD
with gladness; come before Him with joyful singing.
PSALM 100:1–2 NASB

· · ·

A cheerful heart is good medicine,
but a crushed spirit dries up the bones.
PROVERBS 17:22 NIV

Grief can take care of itself, but to get
the full value of a joy you must have
somebody to divide it with.
MARK TWAIN

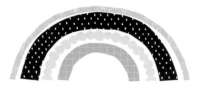

JUSTICE

Maybe you've seen an accused person on the television news, saying, "I demand that justice be served!" Here's a hint for you: Don't ever say that to God. His standards are so high that "justice" for us would be a very painful thing. Thankfully, God is not only just, but merciful—that's why Jesus came to pay the price for our sins. God exemplifies justice to us, and commands that we be just with each other. That's how to serve justice!

"You shall do no injustice in judgment. You shall not be partial to the poor, nor honor the person of the mighty. In righteousness you shall judge your neighbor."
LEVITICUS 19:15 NKJV

• • •

"Do not judge according to appearance, but judge with righteous judgment."
JOHN 7:24 NASB

• • •

"You shall not pervert justice; you shall not show partiality, nor take a bribe, for a bribe blinds the eyes of the wise and twists the words of the righteous. You shall follow what is altogether just, that you may live and inherit the land which the LORD your God is giving you."
DEUTERONOMY 16:19–20 NKJV

• • •

. . .and that no man transgress and defraud his brother in the matter because the Lord is the avenger in all these things, just as we also told you before and solemnly warned you. For God has not called us for the purpose of impurity, but in sanctification. So, he who rejects this is not rejecting man but the God who gives His Holy Spirit to you.
1 THESSALONIANS 4:6–8 NASB

He will judge the world with justice
and rule the nations with fairness.
PSALM 9:8 NLT

. . .

He loveth righteousness and judgment:
the earth is full of the goodness of the LORD.
PSALM 33:5 KJV

. . .

Thus says the LORD: "Execute judgment and
righteousness, and deliver the plundered out of
the hand of the oppressor. Do no wrong and do
no violence to the stranger, the fatherless, or the
widow, nor shed innocent blood in this place."
JEREMIAH 22:3 NKJV

. . .

He will bring forth your righteousness as
the light and your judgment as the noonday.
PSALM 37:6 NASB

. . .

For the LORD is a God of justice.
Blessed are all who wait for him!
ISAIAH 30:18 NIV

. . .

"A bruised reed He will not break, and smoking flax
He will not quench, till He sends forth justice to victory."
MATTHEW 12:20 NKJV

Hate evil, love good, and establish justice in the gate!
AMOS 5:15 NASB

. . .

"I will betroth you to Me forever; yes, I will
betroth you to Me in righteousness and justice,
in lovingkindness and mercy."
HOSEA 2:19 NKJV

. . .

[Jesus] whom God displayed publicly as a propitiation
in His blood through faith. This was to demonstrate His
righteousness, because in the forbearance of God He
passed over the sins previously committed.
ROMANS 3:25 NASB

. . .

Thus speaketh the LORD of hosts, saying,
Execute true judgment, and shew mercy
and compassions every man to his brother.
ZECHARIAH 7:9 KJV

. . .

Blessed are those who keep justice,
and he who does righteousness at all times!
PSALM 106:3 NKJV

. . .

Learn to do good; seek justice, reprove the ruthless,
defend the orphan, plead for the widow.
ISAIAH 1:17 NASB

"O Jacob My servant, do not fear," declares the LORD,
"for I am with you. For I will make a full end of all the
nations where I have driven you, yet I will not make
a full end of you; but I will correct you properly
and by no means leave you unpunished."
JEREMIAH 46:28 NASB

. . .

"Does our law condemn anyone without first
hearing him to find out what he is doing?"
JOHN 7:51 NIV

. . .

"If there is a dispute between men. . .they come to court,
that the judges may judge them, and they justify the
righteous and condemn the wicked."
DEUTERONOMY 25:1 NKJV

. . .

The godly know the rights of the poor;
the wicked don't care to know.
PROVERBS 29:7 NLT

. . .

Moreover I saw under the sun: In the place of judgment,
wickedness was there; and in the place of righteousness,
iniquity was there. I said in my heart, "God shall judge
the righteous and the wicked, for there is a time there
for every purpose and for every work."
ECCLESIASTES 3:16–17 NKJV

It is well with the man who is gracious and lends;
he will maintain his cause in judgment.
PSALM 112:5 NASB

. . .

But if ye had known what this meaneth, I will
have mercy, and not sacrifice, ye would
not have condemned the guiltless.
MATTHEW 12:7 KJV

. . .

"You shall not circulate a false report. Do not put your
hand with the wicked to be an unrighteous witness. You
shall not follow a crowd to do evil; nor shall you testify in
a dispute so as to turn aside after many to pervert justice.
You shall not show partiality to a poor man in his dispute."
EXODUS 23:1–3 NKJV

Never look for righteousness in the other person,
but never cease to be righteous yourself. We are
always looking for justice, yet the essence of
the teaching of the Sermon on the Mount is—
never look for justice, but never cease to give it.
OSWALD CHAMBERS

LABOR

In some circles, it's cool to make fun of work, and to try to get away with as little work as possible. But that attitude is 180 degrees out of phase with God's. Work is an honorable, beneficial thing that, frankly, can keep us out of trouble.

Sure, some jobs can be mundane at times, but remember the One for whom you're ultimately working—it's not just your boss keeping an eye on your efforts. Be thankful for the job God gave you, and work to do the best that you can for His glory.

For the LORD your God will bless you in all
your harvest and in all the work of your hands,
and your joy will be complete.
DEUTERONOMY 16:15 NIV

. . .

Therefore, my beloved brethren, be steadfast,
immovable, always abounding in the work of the Lord,
knowing that your labor is not in vain in the Lord.
1 CORINTHIANS 15:58 NKJV

. . .

When you shall eat of the fruit of your hands,
you will be happy and it will be well with you.
PSALM 128:2 NASB

. . .

Hard work means prosperity;
only fools idle away their time.
PROVERBS 12:11 NLT

. . .

"But you, be strong and do not let your hands
be weak, for your work shall be rewarded!"
2 CHRONICLES 15:7 NKJV

. . .

Do not love sleep, lest you come to poverty;
open your eyes, and you will be satisfied with bread.
PROVERBS 20:13 NKJV

For even when we were with you, we used to
give you this order: if anyone is not willing
to work, then he is not to eat, either.
2 THESSALONIANS 3:10 NASB

. . .

Whatsoever thy hand findeth to do, do it with thy might;
for there is no work, nor device, nor knowledge,
nor wisdom, in the grave, whither thou goest.
ECCLESIASTES 9:10 KJV

. . .

Let the favor of the Lord our God be upon us;
and confirm for us the work of our hands;
yes, confirm the work of our hands.
PSALM 90:17 NASB

. . .

He who has been stealing must steal no longer, but must
work, doing something useful with his own hands, that he
may have something to share with those in need.
EPHESIANS 4:28 NIV

. . .

Six days you shall labor and do all your work, but the
seventh day is the Sabbath of the LORD your God. In it you
shall do no work: you, nor your son, nor your daughter,
nor your male servant, nor your female servant, nor your
cattle, nor your stranger who is within your gates.
EXODUS 20:9–10 NKJV

Make it your ambition to lead a quiet life and attend to
your own business and work with your hands, just as
we commanded you, so that you will behave properly
toward outsiders and not be in any need.
1 THESSALONIANS 4:11–12 NASB

. . .

Then I heard a voice from heaven saying to me, "Write:
'Blessed are the dead who die in the Lord from now on.'"
"Yes," says the Spirit, "that they may rest from their
labors, and their works follow them."
REVELATION 14:13 NKJV

. . .

"For the LORD your God has blessed you in all that you
have done; He has known your wanderings through this
great wilderness. These forty years the LORD your God
has been with you; you have not lacked a thing."
DEUTERONOMY 2:7 NASB

. . .

He becometh poor that dealeth with a slack hand:
but the hand of the diligent maketh rich.
PROVERBS 10:4 KJV

Now he who plants and he who waters are one,
and each one will receive his own reward
according to his own labor.
1 CORINTHIANS 3:8 NKJV

• • •

Do you see a man skilled in his work?
He will stand before kings; he will
not stand before obscure men.
PROVERBS 22:29 NASB

The Son of God reveals Himself in me,
and I serve Him in the ordinary ways
of life out of devotion to Him.

OSWALD CHAMBERS

LOVING GOD

Remember the time Jesus asked Peter, "Do you love Me?" Peter's answer, in modern paraphrase, was, "Yeah, Lord, I love You." Jesus responded, "Feed My sheep," then repeated the exchange two more times. Peter seemed hurt that Jesus would ask him the same question three times, implying that Peter didn't really love Jesus.

It's easy to say that we love God, but it is so much more significant to show that we love Him. Tell God through your actions how much He means to you, and how thankful you are that He is your God.

But from there you will seek the LORD your God,
and you will find Him if you seek Him with
all your heart and with all your soul.
DEUTERONOMY 4:29 NKJV

• • •

The LORD watches over all who love him,
but all the wicked he will destroy.
PSALM 145:20 NIV

• • •

Do not love the world or the things in the world. If anyone
loves the world, the love of the Father is not in him.
1 JOHN 2:15 NKJV

• • •

And we know that God causes all things to work
together for good to those who love God, to those
who are called according to His purpose.
ROMANS 8:28 NASB

• • •

Therefore be imitators of God as dear children.
And walk in love, as Christ also has loved us and
given Himself for us, an offering and a sacrifice
to God for a sweet-smelling aroma.
EPHESIANS 5:1–2 NKJV

"So be very careful to love the LORD your God."
JOSHUA 23:11 NLT

. . .

"I love those who love me; and those
who diligently seek me will find me."
PROVERBS 8:17 NASB

. . .

Jesus said unto them, If God were your Father, ye would
love me: for I proceeded forth and came from God;
neither came I of myself, but he sent me.
JOHN 8:42 KJV

. . .

"And you shall love the LORD your God with all your heart,
with all your soul, with all your mind, and with all your
strength. This is the first commandment."
MARK 12:30 NKJV

. . .

For God is not unjust so as to forget your work
and the love which you have shown toward His name,
in having ministered and in still ministering to the saints.
HEBREWS 6:10 NASB

. . .

Keep yourselves in God's love as you wait for the mercy
of our Lord Jesus Christ to bring you to eternal life.
JUDE 21 NIV

And we have known and believed the love that God has for us. God is love, and he who abides in love abides in God, and God in him. Love has been perfected among us in this: that we may have boldness in the day of judgment; because as He is, so are we in this world. There is no fear in love; but perfect love casts out fear, because fear involves torment. But he who fears has not been made perfect in love. We love Him because He first loved us.
1 JOHN 4:16–19 NKJV

. . .

. . .so that Christ may dwell in your hearts through faith; and that you, being rooted and grounded in love, may be able to comprehend with all the saints what is the breadth and length and height and depth, and to know the love of Christ which surpasses knowledge, that you may be filled up to all the fullness of God.
EPHESIANS 3:17–19 NASB

. . .

"Those who obey my commandments are the ones who love me. And because they love me, my Father will love them, and I will love them. And I will reveal myself to each one of them."
JOHN 14:21 NLT

. . .

But if anyone loves God, he is known by Him.
1 CORINTHIANS 8:3 NASB

"You shall love the LORD your God with all your heart, with all your soul, and with all your strength. And these words which I command you today shall be in your heart."
DEUTERONOMY 6:5–6 NKJV

Today God's eyes are still running all across America, Canada, Mexico, the islands of the sea, the world. . . looking for someone—anyone—who will totally and passionately see Him, who is determined that every thought and action will be pleasing in His sight.
JIM CYMBALA

OBEDIENCE

We send our dogs to "obedience school"—but maybe we should send ourselves. There's just something about submitting to authority that grates on our selfish human natures. But just like Rover at "school," we can earn rewards for obedience, whether from our parents, our government, or most importantly, our God. Demonstrate your love for Him by obeying Him—remember, Jesus said, "If you will obey my commands, you will remain in my love."

If ye keep my commandments, ye shall abide
in my love; even as I have kept my Father's
commandments, and abide in his love.
JOHN 15:10 KJV

. . .

Samuel said, "Has the LORD as much delight
in burnt offerings and sacrifices as in obeying the
voice of the LORD? Behold, to obey is better than
sacrifice, and to heed than the fat of rams."
1 SAMUEL 15:22 NASB

. . .

The things which you learned and received
and heard and saw in me, these do, and the
God of peace will be with you.
PHILIPPIANS 4:9 NKJV

. . .

"If you consent and obey, you will
eat the best of the land."
ISAIAH 1:19 NASB

. . .

Obey your leaders and submit to their authority. They
keep watch over you as men who must give an account.
Obey them so that their work will be a joy, not a burden,
for that would be of no advantage to you.
HEBREWS 13:17 NIV

Let us hear the conclusion of the whole matter: Fear God
and keep His commandments, for this is man's all.
ECCLESIASTES 12:13 NKJV

. . .

"Not everyone who says to Me, 'Lord, Lord,'
will enter the kingdom of heaven, but he who does
the will of My Father who is in heaven will enter."
MATTHEW 7:21 NASB

. . .

"The LORD your God will make you abound in all the
work of your hand, in the fruit of your body, in the
increase of your livestock, and in the produce of your
land for good. For the LORD will again rejoice over
you for good as He rejoiced over your fathers, if you
obey the voice of the LORD your God, to keep His
commandments and His statutes which are written in
this Book of the Law, and if you turn to the LORD your
God with all your heart and with all your soul."
DEUTERONOMY 30:9–10 NKJV

. . .

All the paths of the LORD are mercy and truth unto
such as keep his covenant and his testimonies.
PSALM 25:10 KJV

By this we know that we have come to know Him,
if we keep His commandments. The one who says,
"I have come to know Him," and does not keep His
commandments, is a liar, and the truth is not in him;
but whoever keeps His word, in him the love of God
has truly been perfected. By this we know that we
are in Him: the one who says he abides in Him ought
himself to walk in the same manner as He walked.
1 JOHN 2:3-6 NASB

. . .

Oh, that they had such a heart in them that they would
fear Me and always keep all My commandments, that it
might be well with them and with their children forever!
DEUTERONOMY 5:29 NKJV

. . .

And now, just as you accepted Christ Jesus as your Lord,
you must continue to live in obedience to him. Let your
roots grow down into him and draw up nourishment
from him, so you will grow in faith, strong and vigorous
in the truth you were taught. Let your lives overflow
with thanksgiving for all he has done.
COLOSSIANS 2:6-7 NLT

. . .

"Now that you know these things,
you will be blessed if you do them."
JOHN 13:17 NIV

For not the hearers of the law are just in the sight of God, but the doers of the law will be justified.
ROMANS 2:13 NKJV

. . .

"If they hear and serve Him, they will end their days in prosperity and their years in pleasures."
JOB 36:11 NASB

. . .

But prove yourselves doers of the word, and not merely hearers who delude themselves. For if anyone is a hearer of the word and not a doer, he is like a man who looks at his natural face in a mirror; for once he has looked at himself and gone away, he has immediately forgotten what kind of person he was. But one who looks intently at the perfect law, the law of liberty, and abides by it, not having become a forgetful hearer but an effectual doer, this man will be blessed in what he does.
JAMES 1:22–25 NASB

. . .

And the world is passing away, and the lust of it; but he who does the will of God abides forever.
1 JOHN 2:17 NKJV

. . .

But He said, "More than that, blessed are those who hear the word of God and keep it!"
LUKE 11:28 NKJV

Furthermore, we had earthly fathers to discipline us,
and we respected them; shall we not much rather
be subject to the Father of spirits, and live?
HEBREWS 12:9 NASB

. . .

In that I command thee this day to love the LORD thy God,
to walk in his ways, and to keep his commandments
and his statutes and his judgments, that thou mayest
live and multiply: and the LORD thy God shall bless
thee in the land whither thou goest to possess it.
DEUTERONOMY 30:16 KJV

. . .

Submit yourselves for the Lord's sake to every human
institution, whether to a king as the one in authority,
or to governors as sent by him for the punishment of
evildoers and the praise of those who do right.
1 PETER 2:13–14 NASB

And the person who keeps all of the laws except one is as guilty as the person who has broken all of God's laws.
JAMES 2:10 NLT

. . .

My son, do not forget my teaching, but keep my commands in your heart, for they will prolong your life many years and bring you prosperity.
PROVERBS 3:1–2 NIV

Always remember that when you came to Christ, you became His responsibility. Your part is explicit obedience to everything He tells you to do. His part is covering all the consequences that result from your obedience.
RAY ORTLUND

PATIENCE

You've probably heard that "patience is a virtue." Virtuous or not, what exactly is patience?

For the Christian, patience is more than merely waiting for something to occur; it's a waiting coupled with the right heart attitude—a conscious belief that God is working out His purpose in our lives, no matter how the immediate circumstances appear. Sure, it's easier said than done—but developing patience is one of the best investments you'll ever make in yourself.

He who is slow to anger is better than the mighty,
and he who rules his spirit than he who takes a city.
PROVERBS 16:32 NKJV

. . .

This calls for patient endurance on the part
of the saints who obey God's commandments
and remain faithful to Jesus.
REVELATION 14:12 NIV

. . .

Be humble and gentle. Be patient with each other, making
allowance for each other's faults because of your love.
EPHESIANS 4:2 NLT

. . .

I waited patiently for the LORD; and He
inclined to me, and heard my cry.
PSALM 40:1 NKJV

. . .

. . .knowing that the testing of your faith produces
endurance. And let endurance have its perfect
result, so that you may be perfect and
complete, lacking in nothing.
JAMES 1:3–4 NASB

. . .

That ye be not slothful, but followers of them who
through faith and patience inherit the promises.
HEBREWS 6:12 KJV

The end of a thing is better than its beginning;
the patient in spirit is better than the proud in spirit.
ECCLESIASTES 7:8 NKJV

. . .

Be glad for all God is planning for you.
Be patient in trouble, and always be prayerful.
ROMANS 12:12 NLT

. . .

Be still before the LORD and wait patiently for him; do not
fret when men succeed in their ways, when they carry
out their wicked schemes. . . . For evil men will be cut off,
but those who hope in the LORD will inherit the land.
PSALM 37:7, 9 NIV

. . .

The discretion of a man makes him slow to anger,
and his glory is to overlook a transgression.
PROVERBS 19:11 NKJV

. . .

Therefore be patient, brethren, until the coming of
the Lord. The farmer waits for the precious produce
of the soil, being patient about it, until it gets the
early and late rains. You too be patient; strengthen
your hearts, for the coming of the Lord is near.
JAMES 5:7–8 NASB

Those who control their anger have
great understanding; those with a
hasty temper will make mistakes.
PROVERBS 14:29 NLT

. . .

Now we exhort you, brethren, warn those
who are unruly, comfort the fainthearted,
uphold the weak, be patient with all.
1 THESSALONIANS 5:14 NKJV

I choose patience. . . . I will overlook the
inconveniences of the world. Instead of cursing
the one who takes my place, I'll invite him to do so.
Rather than complain that the wait is too long,
I will thank God for a moment to pray.
MAX LUCADO

PEACE

First day on the new job. . .car breakdown. . .big date Friday night. . .illness in the family. . .there is no shortage of anxiety in our fast-paced, stressful world. But God (that's a great phrase!) has provided peace so that we can rest in Him. God, and only God, can give us the strength and ability to survive, and even thrive among, the pressures of the world. It may be a cliché, but that doesn't make the following quote any less true: "No God, no peace. Know God, know peace."

Be anxious for nothing, but in everything
by prayer and supplication, with thanksgiving,
let your requests be made known to God; and the
peace of God, which surpasses all understanding,
will guard your hearts and minds through Christ Jesus.
PHILIPPIANS 4:6–7 NKJV

. . .

For the mind set on the flesh is death,
but the mind set on the Spirit is life and peace.
ROMANS 8:6 NASB

. . .

Consider the blameless, observe the upright;
there is a future for the man of peace.
PSALM 37:37 NIV

. . .

You will keep him in perfect peace, whose mind
is stayed on You, because he trusts in You.
ISAIAH 26:3 NKJV

. . .

For the Scriptures say, "If you want a happy life and good
days, keep your tongue from speaking evil, and keep your
lips from telling lies. Turn away from evil and do good.
Work hard at living in peace with others."
1 PETER 3:10–11 NLT

So then we pursue the things which make
for peace and the building up of one another.
ROMANS 14:19 NASB

. . .

"Let not your heart be troubled;
you believe in God, believe also in Me."
JOHN 14:1 NKJV

. . .

He who dwells in the shelter of the Most High
will abide in the shadow of the Almighty.
PSALM 91:1 NASB

. . .

Peace I leave with you, my peace I give unto you:
not as the world giveth, give I unto you. Let not
your heart be troubled, neither let it be afraid.
JOHN 14:27 KJV

. . .

Therefore, having been justified by faith, we have
peace with God through our Lord Jesus Christ.
ROMANS 5:1 NKJV

. . .

I will lie down and sleep in peace, for you alone,
O LORD, make me dwell in safety.
PSALM 4:8 NIV

Be at peace among yourselves.
1 THESSALONIANS 5:13 NKJV

. . . .

. . .being diligent to preserve the unity
of the Spirit in the bond of peace.
EPHESIANS 4:3 NASB

. . . .

For the Kingdom of God is not a matter of what
we eat or drink, but of living a life of goodness
and peace and joy in the Holy Spirit.
ROMANS 14:17 NLT

. . . .

Surely He shall deliver you from the snare of the fowler
and from the perilous pestilence. He shall cover you with
His feathers, and under His wings you shall take refuge;
His truth shall be your shield and buckler. You shall not be
afraid of the terror by night, nor of the arrow that flies by
day, nor of the pestilence that walks in darkness, nor of
the destruction that lays waste at noonday.
PSALM 91:3-6 NKJV

. . . .

"Glory to God in the highest, and on earth
peace among men with whom He is pleased."
LUKE 2:14 NASB

Have not I commanded thee? Be strong and of a good courage; be not afraid, neither be thou dismayed: for the Lord thy God is with thee whithersoever thou goest.
JOSHUA 1:9 KJV

. . .

Turn from evil and do good; seek peace and pursue it.
PSALM 34:14 NIV

. . .

And let the peace of God rule in your hearts, to which also you were called in one body; and be thankful.
COLOSSIANS 3:15 NKJV

. . .

A thousand may fall at your side, and ten thousand at your right hand; but it shall not come near you. Only with your eyes shall you look, and see the reward of the wicked. Because you have made the LORD, who is my refuge, even the Most High, your dwelling place, no evil shall befall you, nor shall any plague come near your dwelling.
PSALM 91:7–10 NKJV

. . .

God has called us to peace.
1 CORINTHIANS 7:15 NASB

First of all, then, I urge that entreaties and prayers,
petitions and thanksgivings, be made on behalf of all men,
for kings and all who are in authority, so that we may lead
a tranquil and quiet life in all godliness and dignity.
1 TIMOTHY 2:1–2 NASB

. . .

Do your part to live in peace with everyone,
as much as possible.
ROMANS 12:18 NLT

. . .

The LORD will give strength to His people;
the LORD will bless His people with peace.
PSALM 29:11 NKJV

. . .

"Blessed are the peacemakers,
for they shall be called sons of God."
MATTHEW 5:9 NASB

. . .

Deceit is in the heart of them that imagine evil:
but to the counsellors of peace is joy.
PROVERBS 12:20 KJV

. . .

Now the fruit of righteousness is sown
in peace by those who make peace.
JAMES 3:18 NKJV

Those who love Your law have great peace,
and nothing causes them to stumble.
PSALM 119:165 NASB

. . .

Make every effort to live in peace with
all men and to be holy; without holiness
no one will see the Lord.
HEBREWS 12:14 NIV

There is a way to inner peace but it isn't through
our own sophistication, abilities, talents,
or internal makeup; it is through God.
ROGER PALMS

PERSEVERANCE

A handful of people are born with tremendous gifts—athletic skills, musical talents, intellectual abilities—and seem destined to succeed. But what about the rest of us? The normal people who test out average? The key to our success is perseverance, hard work in the face of every obstacle—that quality that previous generations called "stick-to-it-iveness." Perseverance is a great trait to develop in life—and especially in our spiritual lives. God wants marathon runners, not sprinters!

To those who by persistence in doing good seek glory,
honor and immortality, he will give eternal life.
ROMANS 2:7 NIV

. . .

Yet I am not ashamed, because I know whom
I have believed, and am convinced that he is able
to guard what I have entrusted to him for that day.
What you heard from me, keep as the pattern of
sound teaching, with faith and love in Christ Jesus.
2 TIMOTHY 1:12–13 NIV

. . .

Then Jesus said to those Jews who believed Him,
"If you abide in My word, you are My disciples indeed."
JOHN 8:31 NKJV

. . .

Here is the perseverance of the saints who keep the
commandments of God and their faith in Jesus.
REVELATION 14:12 NASB

. . .

God blesses the people who patiently endure testing.
Afterward they will receive the crown of life that
God has promised to those who love him.
JAMES 1:12 NLT

You therefore must endure hardship
as a good soldier of Jesus Christ.
2 TIMOTHY 2:3 NKJV

. . .

Whatever you do, do your work heartily, as for
the Lord rather than for men, knowing that
from the Lord you will receive the reward of the
inheritance. It is the Lord Christ whom you serve.
COLOSSIANS 3:23–24 NASB

. . .

And let us not be weary in well doing:
for in due season we shall reap, if we faint not.
GALATIANS 6:9 KJV

. . .

And not only that, but we also glory in tribulations,
knowing that tribulation produces perseverance;
and perseverance, character; and character, hope.
ROMANS 5:3–4 NKJV

. . .

Let us hold fast the confession of our hope without
wavering, for He who promised is faithful.
HEBREWS 10:23 NASB

. . .

May the Lord direct your hearts into
God's love and Christ's perseverance.
2 THESSALONIANS 3:5 NIV

You therefore, beloved, since you know this beforehand,
beware lest you also fall from your own steadfastness,
being led away with the error of the wicked.
2 PETER 3:17 NKJV

. . .

For we have become partakers of Christ, if we hold fast
the beginning of our assurance firm until the end.
HEBREWS 3:14 NASB

. . .

"I will invite everyone who is victorious to sit
with me on my throne, just as I was victorious
and sat with my Father on his throne."
REVELATION 3:21 NLT

. . .

Stand fast therefore in the liberty by which
Christ has made us free, and do not be
entangled again with a yoke of bondage.
GALATIANS 5:1 NKJV

. . .

Everyone who competes in the games exercises
self-control in all things. They then do it to receive a
perishable wreath, but we an imperishable. Therefore
I run in such a way, as not without aim; I box in such
a way, as not beating the air; but I discipline my body
and make it my slave, so that, after I have preached
to others, I myself will not be disqualified.
1 CORINTHIANS 9:25–27 NASB

I can do all things through Christ who strengthens me.
PHILIPPIANS 4:13 NKJV

· · ·

I have fought a good fight, I have finished my course,
I have kept the faith: Henceforth there is laid up for me
a crown of righteousness, which the Lord, the righteous
judge, shall give me at that day: and not to me only,
but unto all them also that love his appearing.
2 TIMOTHY 4:7–8 KJV

· · ·

Therefore we also, since we are surrounded by so
great a cloud of witnesses, let us lay aside every
weight, and the sin which so easily ensnares us,
and let us run with endurance the race that is set
before us, looking unto Jesus, the author and finisher
of our faith, who for the joy that was set before
Him endured the cross, despising the shame, and has
sat down at the right hand of the throne of God.
HEBREWS 12:1–2 NKJV

I think and think for months and years,
ninety-nine times, the conclusion is false.
The hundredth time I am right.
ALBERT EINSTEIN

PHYSICAL CARE

True or false: Working out makes you a better person.

Well, exercise may make you a better person physically—you'll probably look better and feel better about yourself. It is wise to take care of the body that God gave you. But even though physical care is necessary, it's not nearly as important as spiritual care—so make sure you've got your priorities in the proper order. Running a five-minute mile is great—but spending five minutes in God's Word is even better.

For bodily discipline is only of little profit, but godliness
is profitable for all things, since it holds promise for
the present life and also for the life to come.
1 TIMOTHY 4:8 NASB

. . .

Do you not know that your body is a temple of the
Holy Spirit, who is in you, whom you have received
from God? You are not your own; you were bought
at a price. Therefore honor God with your body.
1 CORINTHIANS 6:19–20 NIV

. . .

You do not know what will happen tomorrow. For what
is your life? It is even a vapor that appears for a little
time and then vanishes away. Instead you ought to say,
"If the Lord wills, we shall live and do this or that."
JAMES 4:14–15 NKJV

. . .

"Do not fear those who kill the body but are
unable to kill the soul; but rather fear Him who
is able to destroy both soul and body in hell."
MATTHEW 10:28 NASB

. . .

"Do not judge according to appearance,
but judge with righteous judgment."
JOHN 7:24 NKJV

But the LORD said unto Samuel, Look not on
his countenance, or on the height of his stature;
because I have refused him: for the LORD seeth
not as man seeth; for man looketh on the outward
appearance, but the LORD looketh on the heart.
1 SAMUEL 16:7 KJV

. . .

And so, dear brothers and sisters, I plead with
you to give your bodies to God. Let them be a living
and holy sacrifice—the kind he will accept. When you
think of what he has done for you, is this too much
to ask? Don't copy the behavior and customs of this
world, but let God transform you into a new person by
changing the way you think. Then you will know what
God wants you to do, and you will know how good and
pleasing and perfect his will really is. As God's messenger,
I give each of you this warning: Be honest in your
estimate of yourselves, measuring your value
by how much faith God has given you.
ROMANS 12:1–3 NLT

. . .

Therefore, from now on, we regard no one according to
the flesh. Even though we have known Christ according to
the flesh, yet now we know Him thus no longer. Therefore,
if anyone is in Christ, he is a new creation; old things have
passed away; behold, all things have become new.
2 CORINTHIANS 5:16–17 NKJV

Beloved, I pray that in all respects you may prosper and be in good health, just as your soul prospers.
3 JOHN 2 NASB

. . .

Likewise, I want women to adorn themselves with proper clothing, modestly and discreetly, not with braided hair and gold or pearls or costly garments, but rather by means of good works, as is proper for women making a claim to godliness.
1 TIMOTHY 2:9–10 NASB

. . .

If you show special attention to the man wearing fine clothes and say, "Here's a good seat for you," but say to the poor man, "You stand there" or "Sit on the floor by my feet," have you not discriminated among yourselves and become judges with evil thoughts?
JAMES 2:3–4 NIV

My deeds will not be measured by my youthful appearance, but by the concern lines on my forehead and the laugh lines around my mouth.
ERMA BOMBECK

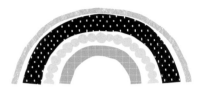

PRAYER

Sometimes the whole concept is hard to grasp: The holy, all-powerful God actually wants us to talk to Him. It's called prayer.

Although God knows what you will say even before you do, He still waits for you to enter His presence in prayer. No request is too large (or too small!) to take before Him. God loves you, and wants to answer your prayers. Have a hard time believing that? Then read the following verses!

Therefore I want the men in every place to pray,
lifting up holy hands, without wrath and dissension.
1 TIMOTHY 2:8 NASB

• • •

"If you sinful people know how to give good gifts to
your children, how much more will your heavenly
Father give good gifts to those who ask him."
MATTHEW 7:11 NLT

• • •

The LORD is near to all who call upon Him,
to all who call upon Him in truth.
PSALM 145:18 NKJV

• • •

In the same way the Spirit also helps our weakness;
for we do not know how to pray as we should,
but the Spirit Himself intercedes for us with
groanings too deep for words.
ROMANS 8:26 NASB

• • •

Then shall ye call upon me, and ye shall go and
pray unto me, and I will hearken unto you.
JEREMIAH 29:12 KJV

• • •

He shall call upon Me, and I will answer him; I will be
with him in trouble; I will deliver him and honor him.
PSALM 91:15 NKJV

"Until now you have asked for nothing in My name; ask
and you will receive, so that your joy may be made full."
JOHN 16:24 NASB

. . .

The LORD detests the sacrifice of the wicked,
but the prayer of the upright pleases him.
PROVERBS 15:8 NIV

. . .

"We will give ourselves continually to
prayer and to the ministry of the word."
ACTS 6:3–4 NKJV

. . .

"It will also come to pass that before they call,
I will answer; and while they are
still speaking, I will hear."
ISAIAH 65:24 NASB

. . .

Morning, noon, and night I plead aloud in
my distress, and the LORD hears my voice.
PSALM 55:17 NLT

. . .

You will make your prayer to Him,
He will hear you, and you will pay your vows.
JOB 22:27 NKJV

"Ask, and it will be given to you; seek, and you will find; knock, and it will be opened to you."
MATTHEW 7:7 NKJV

. . .

For this shall every one that is godly pray unto thee in a time when thou mayest be found: surely in the floods of great waters they shall not come nigh unto him.
PSALM 32:6 KJV

. . .

Be anxious for nothing, but in everything by prayer and supplication with thanksgiving let your requests be made known to God. And the peace of God, which surpasses all comprehension, will guard your hearts and your minds in Christ Jesus.
PHILIPPIANS 4:6–7 NASB

. . .

Therefore, confess your sins to one another, and pray for one another so that you may be healed. The effective prayer of a righteous man can accomplish much.
JAMES 5:16 NASB

. . .

But I pray to you, O LORD, in the time of your favor; in your great love, O God, answer me with your sure salvation.
PSALM 69:13 NIV

. . .praying always with all prayer and supplication
in the Spirit, being watchful to this end with all
perseverance and supplication for all the saints.
EPHESIANS 6:18 NKJV

• • •

Then he will pray to God, and He will accept him,
that he may see His face with joy, and He may
restore His righteousness to man.
JOB 33:26 NASB

• • •

"But when you pray, go away by yourself, shut the door
behind you, and pray to your Father secretly. Then your
Father, who knows all secrets, will reward you. When
you pray, don't babble on and on as people of other
religions do. They think their prayers are answered
only by repeating their words again and again."
MATTHEW 6:6–7 NLT

• • •

Rejoicing in hope, persevering
in tribulation, devoted to prayer. . .
ROMANS 12:12 NASB

• • •

For the people shall dwell in Zion at Jerusalem; you shall
weep no more. He will be very gracious to you at the
sound of your cry; when He hears it, He will answer you.
ISAIAH 30:19 NKJV

What is the outcome then? I will pray with the spirit
and I will pray with the mind also; I will sing with
the spirit and I will sing with the mind also.
1 CORINTHIANS 14:15 NASB

. . .

I waited patiently for the LORD; and he
inclined unto me, and heard my cry.
PSALM 40:1 KJV

. . .

"Again I say to you that if two of you agree
on earth concerning anything that they ask,
it will be done for them by My Father in heaven.
For where two or three are gathered together
in My name, I am there in the midst of them."
MATTHEW 18:19–20 NKJV

. . .

Let us then approach the throne of grace with
confidence, so that we may receive mercy and
find grace to help us in our time of need.
HEBREWS 4:16 NIV

. . .

Now this is the confidence that we have in Him, that if
we ask anything according to His will, He hears us. And
if we know that He hears us, whatever we ask, we know
that we have the petitions that we have asked of Him.
1 JOHN 5:14–15 NKJV

The prayer offered in faith will restore the one who is sick, and the Lord will raise him up, and if he has committed sins, they will be forgiven him.
JAMES 5:15 NASB

. . .

O LORD, hear me as I pray; pay attention to my groaning. Listen to my cry for help, my King and my God, for I will never pray to anyone but you. Listen to my voice in the morning, LORD.
PSALM 5:1–3 NLT

. . .

"And whatever things you ask in prayer, believing, you will receive."
MATTHEW 21:22 NKJV

. . .

Pray without ceasing; in everything give thanks; for this is God's will for you in Christ Jesus.
1 THESSALONIANS 5:17–18 NASB

Prayer is in very deed the pulse of the spiritual life. It is the great means of bringing to minister and people the blessing and power of heaven. Persevering and believing prayer means a strong and an abundant life.
ANDREW MURRAY

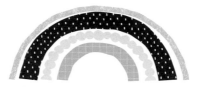

PURITY

In a sex-crazy world, purity seems like a horribly outdated idea. You certainly won't find much support for it in movies, TV shows, or pop music. But the Christian faith is truly counter-cultural—and purity means a lot. Not only to God, either—what greater gift could a person give his or her future spouse than the gift of purity? When you choose to remain pure, you avoid the dangers of pregnancy, disease, and guilt, and give yourself a much greater chance of having a long-lasting, happy marriage. Old-fashioned? Yes—but it works!

For this is the will of God, your sanctification: that you should abstain from sexual immorality; that each of you should know how to possess his own vessel in sanctification and honor, not in passion of lust, like the Gentiles who do not know God. . . . For God did not call us to uncleanness, but in holiness.
1 THESSALONIANS 4:3–5, 7 NKJV

. . .

Do you not know that your bodies are members of Christ? Shall I then take away the members of Christ and make them members of a prostitute? May it never be! Or do you not know that the one who joins himself to a prostitute is one body with her? For He says, "The two shall become one flesh." But the one who joins himself to the Lord is one spirit with Him. Flee immorality. Every other sin that a man commits is outside the body, but the immoral man sins against his own body. Or do you not know that your body is a temple of the Holy Spirit who is in you, whom you have from God, and that you are not your own? For you have been bought with a price: therefore glorify God in your body.
1 CORINTHIANS 6:15–20 NASB

. . .

But put on the Lord Jesus Christ, and make no provision for the flesh, to fulfill its lusts.
ROMANS 13:14 NKJV

For all that is in the world—the lust of the flesh, the lust of the eyes, and the pride of life—is not of the Father but is of the world. And the world is passing away, and the lust of it; but he who does the will of God abides forever.
1 JOHN 2:16–17 NKJV

. . .

Be imitators of God, therefore, as dearly loved children and live a life of love, just as Christ loved us and gave himself up for us as a fragrant offering and sacrifice to God. But among you there must not be even a hint of sexual immorality, or of any kind of impurity, or of greed, because these are improper for God's holy people.
EPHESIANS 5:1–3 NIV

. . .

Now concerning the things about which you wrote, it is good for a man not to touch a woman. But because of immoralities, each man is to have his own wife, and each woman is to have her own husband.
1 CORINTHIANS 7:1–2 NASB

. . .

Finally, brethren, whatever is true, whatever is honorable, whatever is right, whatever is pure, whatever is lovely, whatever is of good repute, if there is any excellence and if anything worthy of praise, dwell on these things.
PHILIPPIANS 4:8 NASB

But I say unto you, That whosoever looketh on
a woman to lust after her hath committed
adultery with her already in his heart.
MATTHEW 5:28 KJV

. . .

"I have made a covenant with my eyes;
why then should I look upon a young woman?"
JOB 31:1NKJV

. . .

Now those who belong to Christ Jesus have
crucified the flesh with its passions and desires.
GALATIANS 5:24 NASB

. . .

The body is not meant for sexual immorality,
but for the Lord, and the Lord for the body.
1 CORINTHIANS 6:13 NIV

. . .

So I advise you to live according to your
new life in the Holy Spirit. Then you won't
be doing what your sinful nature craves.
GALATIANS 5:16 NLT

Therefore put to death your members which are
on the earth: fornication, uncleanness, passion,
evil desire, and covetousness, which is idolatry.
Because of these things the wrath of God is
coming upon the sons of disobedience.
COLOSSIANS 3:5–6 NKJV

Chastity, abstinence—saving sex for marriage—
is not for wimps! . . . Sexual activity does not make a
boy a man or a girl a woman. But sexual activity outside
of marriage can ruin a person's life and the lives of
others. It takes a real man or woman to make tough
choices they won't regret later. . .to stand up to the
pressure when it seems like everyone else is "doing it."

LINDA BARTLETT

RELATIONSHIPS

"Relationships" is one of those multipurpose words. It can cover your friendships, your family ties, and your church connections. Those "relationships" are made up of special people who share your happiness and your pain. They're the people who laugh with you, listen to you when you need to talk, pray with you, encourage you, and support you through adversity. God knew that you would need that kind of support, so He gave you relationships. Thank Him for the ones He's brought into your life.

Now may the God who gives perseverance and
encouragement grant you to be of the same mind
with one another according to Christ Jesus.
ROMANS 15:5 NASB

. . .

"Honor your father and mother." This is the first of the
Ten Commandments that ends with a promise. And this
is the promise: If you honor your father and mother,
"you will live a long life, full of blessing."
EPHESIANS 6:2–3 NLT

. . .

For all the law is fulfilled in one word, even in this:
"You shall love your neighbor as yourself."
GALATIANS 5:14 NKJV

. . .

Finally, all of you, live in harmony with one
another; be sympathetic, love as brothers,
be compassionate and humble.
1 PETER 3:8 NIV

. . .

"Therefore, if you are offering your gift at the altar
and there remember that your brother has something
against you, leave your gift there in front of the altar.
First go and be reconciled to your brother;
then come and offer your gift."
MATTHEW 5:23–24 NIV

If you really fulfill the royal law according to the Scripture,
"You shall love your neighbor as yourself," you do well.
JAMES 2:8 NKJV

• • •

"You shall not take vengeance, nor bear any grudge
against the sons of your people, but you shall love
your neighbor as yourself; I am the LORD."
LEVITICUS 19:18 NASB

• • •

Anyone who hates his brother is a murderer,
and you know that no murderer has eternal life in him.
1 JOHN 3:15 NIV

• • •

But love your enemies, do good, and lend, hoping
for nothing in return; and your reward will be great,
and you will be sons of the Most High. For He is
kind to the unthankful and evil. Therefore be
merciful, just as your Father also is merciful.
LUKE 6:35–36 NKJV

• • •

"You have heard that it was said, 'You shall love your
neighbor and hate your enemy.' But I say to you, love
your enemies and pray for those who persecute you,
so that you may be sons of your Father who is in heaven;
for He causes His sun to rise on the evil and the good,
and sends rain on the righteous and the unrighteous."
MATTHEW 5:43–45 NASB

When others are happy, be happy with them.
If they are sad, share their sorrow.
ROMANS 12:15 NLT

. . .

Now the fruit of righteousness is sown
in peace by those who make peace.
JAMES 3:18 NKJV

. . .

Bear one another's burdens,
and thereby fulfill the law of Christ.
GALATIANS 6:2 NASB

. . .

Beloved, let us love one another: for love is of God; and
every one that loveth is born of God, and knoweth God.
1 JOHN 4:7 KJV

. . .

So speak and so do as those who will be judged by the law
of liberty. For judgment is without mercy to the one who
has shown no mercy. Mercy triumphs over judgment.
JAMES 2:12–13 NKJV

. . .

Owe nothing to anyone except to love one another;
for he who loves his neighbor has fulfilled the law.
ROMANS 13:8 NASB

Though I speak with the tongues of men and of angels, and have not charity, I am become as sounding brass, or a tinkling cymbal. And though I have the gift of prophecy, and understand all mysteries, and all knowledge; and though I have all faith, so that I could remove mountains, and have not charity, I am nothing. And though I bestow all my goods to feed the poor, and though I give my body to be burned, and have not charity, it profiteth me nothing.

1 CORINTHIANS 13:1–3 KJV

. . . .

"This is My commandment, that you love one another as I have loved you. Greater love has no one than this, than to lay down one's life for his friends."

JOHN 15:12–13 NKJV

. . . .

For this is the message which you have heard from the beginning, that we should love one another.

1 JOHN 3:11 NASB

. . . .

Don't team up with those who are unbelievers. How can goodness be a partner with wickedness? How can light live with darkness?

2 CORINTHIANS 6:14 NLT

. . . .

Honor all people. Love the brotherhood. Fear God. Honor the king.

1 PETER 2:17 NKJV

Be subject to one another in the fear of Christ.
EPHESIANS 5:21 NASB

. . .

Be kindly affectioned one to another with brotherly love;
in honour preferring one another.
ROMANS 12:10 KJV

. . .

Beloved, if God so loved us, we also ought to love
one another. No one has seen God at any time.
If we love one another, God abides in us,
and His love has been perfected in us.
1 JOHN 4:11–12 NKJV

. . .

Love is patient, love is kind and is not jealous;
love does not brag and is not arrogant, does not act
unbecomingly; it does not seek its own, is not provoked,
does not take into account a wrong suffered.
1 CORINTHIANS 13:4–5 NASB

I cannot even imagine where I would be today were it not
for that handful of friends who have given me a heart full
of joy. Let's face it—friends make life a lot more fun.
CHARLES SWINDOLL

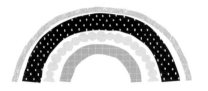

REPENTANCE

Admittedly, it's not fun. Repentance can even be painful—when you recognize that you have sinned against your heavenly Father, and need to ask His forgiveness. But, as the old workout motto goes, "No pain, no gain." When you do your part by repenting, God does His part by forgiving. He doesn't hold those faults against you, and you've got a clean slate before Him. Easy? No. Worthwhile? Definitely. Is there anything you should repent of today?

Therefore, confess your sins to one another, and pray
for one another so that you may be healed. The effective
prayer of a righteous man can accomplish much.
JAMES 5:16 NASB

. . .

"But go and learn what this means:
'I desire mercy, not sacrifice.' For I have
not come to call the righteous, but sinners."
MATTHEW 9:13 NIV

. . .

The sacrifices of God are a broken spirit, a broken and
a contrite heart—these, O God, You will not despise.
PSALM 51:17 NKJV

. . .

"But if wicked people turn away from all their sins and
begin to obey my laws and do what is just and right,
they will surely live and not die. All their past sins will
be forgotten, and they will live because of the righteous
things they have done. Do you think, asks the Sovereign
Lord, that I like to see wicked people die? Of course not!
I only want them to turn from their wicked ways and live."
EZEKIEL 18:21–23 NLT

. . .

The LORD has heard my supplication;
the LORD will receive my prayer.
PSALM 6:9 NKJV

"If you return to the Almighty, you will be restored;
if you remove unrighteousness far from your tent."
JOB 22:23 NASB

. . .

Wherefore I say unto you, All manner of sin and
blasphemy shall be forgiven unto men: but the blasphemy
against the Holy Ghost shall not be forgiven unto men.
MATTHEW 12:31 KJV

. . .

Draw near to God and He will draw near to you.
Cleanse your hands, you sinners; and purify
your hearts, you double-minded.
JAMES 4:8 NKJV

. . .

He who conceals his transgressions will
not prosper, but he who confesses and
forsakes them will find compassion.
PROVERBS 28:13 NASB

. . .

"God. . .commands all people everywhere to repent."
ACTS 17:30 NIV

. . .

The LORD is close to the brokenhearted;
he rescues those who are crushed in spirit.
PSALM 34:18 NLT

Or do you think lightly of the riches of His kindness
and tolerance and patience, not knowing that the
kindness of God leads you to repentance?
ROMANS 2:4 NASB

. . .

Seek the LORD while He may be found, call upon
Him while He is near. Let the wicked forsake his way,
and the unrighteous man his thoughts; let him return
to the LORD, and He will have mercy on him; and to
our God, for He will abundantly pardon.
ISAIAH 55:6–7 NKJV

. . .

If we confess our sins, He is faithful and just to forgive us
our sins and to cleanse us from all unrighteousness.
1 JOHN 1:9 NKJV

. . .

For they themselves report about us what kind of a
reception we had with you, and how you turned to God
from idols to serve a living and true God, and to wait for
His Son from heaven, whom He raised from the dead,
that is Jesus, who rescues us from the wrath to come.
1 THESSALONIANS 1:9–10 NASB

. . .

"The time is fulfilled, and the kingdom of God
is at hand; repent and believe in the gospel."
MARK 1:15 NASB

And rend your heart, and not your garments,
and turn unto the LORD your God: for he is
gracious and merciful, slow to anger, and of
great kindness, and repenteth him of the evil.
JOEL 2:13 KJV

. . .

"Therefore repent of this wickedness of yours,
and pray the Lord that, if possible, the intention
of your heart may be forgiven you."
ACTS 8:22 NASB

. . .

"But at last my people will confess their sins and the sins
of their ancestors for betraying me and being hostile
toward me. Finally, when I have given full expression
to my hostility and have brought them to the land of
their enemies, then at last their disobedient hearts will
be humbled, and they will pay for their sins. Then I
will remember my covenant with Jacob, with Isaac,
and with Abraham, and I will remember the land."
LEVITICUS 26:40–42 NLT

. . .

I acknowledged my sin to You, and my iniquity I have not
hidden. I said, "I will confess my transgressions to the
LORD," and You forgave the iniquity of my sin.
PSALM 32:5 NKJV

"So remember what you have received and heard; and keep it, and repent. Therefore if you do not wake up, I will come like a thief, and you will not know at what hour I will come to you."
REVELATION 3:3 NASB

• • •

Speak unto the children of Israel, When a man or woman shall commit any sin that men commit, to do a trespass against the LORD, and that person be guilty; Then they shall confess their sin which they have done: and he shall recompense his trespass with the principal thereof, and add unto it the fifth part thereof, and give it unto him against whom he hath trespassed.
NUMBERS 5:6–7 KJV

• • •

"Then he will pray to God, and He will accept him, that he may see His face with joy, and He may restore His righteousness to man."
JOB 33:26 NASB

• • •

Repent ye therefore, and be converted, that your sins may be blotted out, when the times of refreshing shall come from the presence of the Lord.
ACTS 3:19 KJV

"Repent, for the kingdom of heaven is at hand!"
MATTHEW 3:2 NKJV

. . .

"In the same way, I tell you, there is
rejoicing in the presence of the angels
of God over one sinner who repents."
LUKE 15:10 NIV

. . .

Who may ascend into the hill of the LORD? Or who may
stand in His holy place? He who has clean hands and a
pure heart, who has not lifted up his soul to an idol, nor
sworn deceitfully. He shall receive blessing from the LORD,
and righteousness from the God of his salvation.
PSALM 24:3–5 NKJV

Repentance may be old-fashioned,
but it is not outdated so long as there is sin.
J. C. MACAULAY

RESPONSIBILITY

"I have my rights!" people like to say. What they generally overlook are their responsibilities—those duties and obligations of family life, citizenship, or any group membership. For Christians, that responsibility is to conduct their lives in the way that God desires and expects. Responsibility may not always seem fun, but it is the sign of maturity. There are choices to be made daily that require a spiritual readiness. Live your life prepared to make the right choices, never to be caught off-guard by Satan's schemes.

"I will give to each one of you according to your deeds."
REVELATION 2:23 NASB

. . .

In everything you do, stay away from complaining
and arguing, so that no one can speak a word of
blame against you. You are to live clean, innocent
lives as children of God in a dark world full of crooked
and perverse people. Let your lives shine brightly
before them. Hold tightly to the word of life, so that
when Christ returns, I will be proud that I did not lose
the race and that my work was not useless.
PHILIPPIANS 2:14–16 NLT

. . .

Dearly beloved, I beseech you as strangers and pilgrims,
abstain from fleshly lusts, which war against the soul;
Having your conversation honest among the Gentiles:
that, whereas they speak against you as evildoers, they
may by your good works, which they shall behold, glorify
God in the day of visitation. Submit yourselves to every
ordinance of man for the Lord's sake: whether it be to the
king, as supreme; Or unto governors, as unto them that
are sent by him for the punishment of evildoers, and for
the praise of them that do well. For so is the will of God,
that with well doing ye may put to silence the ignorance
of foolish men: As free, and not using your liberty for a
cloke of maliciousness, but as the servants of God.
1 PETER 2:11–16 KJV

And they were both righteous before God,
walking in all the commandments and
ordinances of the Lord blameless.
LUKE 1:6 NKJV

. . .

"Therefore I will judge you, O house of Israel, each
according to his conduct," declares the Lord GOD.
"Repent and turn away from all your transgressions, so
that iniquity may not become a stumbling block to you."
EZEKIEL 18:30 NASB

. . .

But let each one examine his own work, and then
he will have rejoicing in himself alone, and not in
another. For each one shall bear his own load.
GALATIANS 6:4–5 NKJV

*You cannot escape the responsibility
of tomorrow by evading it today.*
ABRAHAM LINCOLN

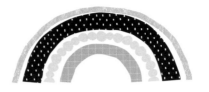

SALVATION

Quick—what's the most important thing in your life? Your boyfriend or best friend? Your new car? Your family? Your degree? If you're a Christian, the answer should be this: your salvation. God has offered salvation, to all who will accept it, as a free gift. It's free, but not cheap—salvation required the sacrifice of God's only Son, Jesus Christ, on the cross. Why not take a minute to thank God for His gift, and for the person who shared the gift of salvation with you? Then go out and share the gift with others.

For by grace you have been saved through faith,
and that not of yourselves; it is the gift of God.
EPHESIANS 2:8 NKJV

. . .

"Therefore let it be known to you, brethren, that through
Him forgiveness of sins is proclaimed to you."
ACTS 13:38 NASB

. . .

My dear children, I am writing this to you so that you will
not sin. But if you do sin, there is someone to plead for
you before the Father. He is Jesus Christ, the one who
pleases God completely. He is the sacrifice for our sins.
He takes away not only our sins but the sins of all the world.
1 JOHN 2:1–2 NLT

. . .

God made him who had no sin to be sin for us, so that
in him we might become the righteousness of God.
2 CORINTHIANS 5:21 NIV

. . .

"Nor is there salvation in any other, for there
is no other name under heaven given among
men by which we must be saved."
ACTS 4:12 NKJV

He who believes and is baptized will be saved;
but he who does not believe will be condemned.
MARK 16:16 NKJV

. . .

Jesus answered and said to him, "Truly, truly, I say
to you, unless one is born again he cannot see the
kingdom of God." Nicodemus said to Him, "How can a
man be born when he is old? He cannot enter a second
time into his mother's womb and be born, can he?"
Jesus answered, "Truly, truly, I say to you, unless one
is born of water and the Spirit he cannot enter into the
kingdom of God. That which is born of the flesh is flesh,
and that which is born of the Spirit is spirit. Do not be
amazed that I said to you, 'You must be born again.' "
JOHN 3:3–7 NASB

. . .

"Look! Here I stand at the door and knock. If you
hear me calling and open the door, I will come in,
and we will share a meal as friends."
REVELATION 3:20 NLT

. . .

For this is good and acceptable in the sight of
God our Savior, who desires all men to be saved
and to come to the knowledge of the truth.
1 TIMOTHY 2:3–4 NKJV

. . .

But to all who believed him and accepted him,
he gave the right to become children of God. They
are reborn! This is not a physical birth resulting from
human passion or plan—this rebirth comes from God.
JOHN 1:12–13 NLT

. . .

"I tell you that in the same way, there will be more
joy in heaven over one sinner who repents than over
ninety-nine righteous persons who need no repentance."
LUKE 15:7 NASB

. . .

If you confess with your mouth Jesus as Lord, and believe
in your heart that God raised Him from the dead, you will
be saved; for with the heart a person believes, resulting in
righteousness, and with the mouth he confesses, resulting
in salvation. For the Scripture says, "Whoever believes in
Him will not be disappointed." For there is no distinction
between Jew and Greek; for the same Lord is Lord of all,
abounding in riches for all who call on Him; for "Whoever
will call on the name of the Lord will be saved."
ROMANS 10:9–13 NASB

. . .

"He who believes in Him is not condemned;
but he who does not believe is condemned
already, because he has not believed in the
name of the only begotten Son of God."
JOHN 3:18 NKJV

"I am the door; if anyone enters through Me, he will be saved, and will go in and out and find pasture."
JOHN 10:9 NASB

• • •

But when the kindness and the love of God our Savior toward man appeared, not by works of righteousness which we have done, but according to His mercy He saved us, through the washing of regeneration and renewing of the Holy Spirit, whom He poured out on us abundantly through Jesus Christ our Savior.
TITUS 3:4–6 NKJV

• • •

"He who believes in the Son has eternal life; but he who does not obey the Son will not see life, but the wrath of God abides on him."
JOHN 3:36 NASB

• • •

And they said, Believe on the Lord Jesus Christ, and thou shalt be saved, and thy house.
ACTS 16:31 KJV

• • •

Therefore, if anyone is in Christ, he is a new creation; old things have passed away; behold, all things have become new.
2 CORINTHIANS 5:17 NKJV

"I give eternal life to them, and they will never perish; and no one will snatch them out of My hand."
JOHN 10:28 NASB

. . .

"Enter through the narrow gate. For wide is the gate and broad is the road that leads to destruction, and many enter through it. But small is the gate and narrow the road that leads to life, and only a few find it."
MATTHEW 7:13–14 NIV

. . .

Therefore lay aside all filthiness and overflow of wickedness, and receive with meekness the implanted word, which is able to save your souls.
JAMES 1:21 NKJV

Each person must decide for or against Christ. Turning our backs—or even just ignoring the question—results in living in darkness.
JIM GRASSI

SCRIPTURE

Ever wish that life had an owner's manual, like your car or your computer do? Well, life does—it's called the Bible. God's Word is the Christian's manual for a happy and productive life—but only if it's used properly. Take the Bible off your shelf, and read it every day. Memorize important scriptures, and bring them to mind when trouble or temptation strikes. God's Word can bring comfort and strength when you need them most.

Let the word of Christ richly dwell within you,
with all wisdom teaching and admonishing one
another with psalms and hymns and spiritual songs,
singing with thankfulness in your hearts to God.
COLOSSIANS 3:16 NASB

. . .

I have hidden your word in my heart,
that I might not sin against you.
PSALM 119:11 NLT

. . .

But you must continue in the things which you have
learned and been assured of, knowing from whom you
have learned them, and that from childhood you have
known the Holy Scriptures, which are able to make you
wise for salvation through faith which is in Christ Jesus.
2 TIMOTHY 3:14–15 NKJV

. . .

You should remember the words spoken beforehand
by the holy prophets and the commandment of
the Lord and Savior spoken by your apostles.
2 PETER 3:2 NASB

. . .

Your word is a lamp to my feet and a light for my path.
PSALM 119:105 NIV

So shall my word be that goeth forth out of my mouth: it shall not return unto me void, but it shall accomplish that which I please, and it shall prosper in the thing whereto I sent it.
ISAIAH 55:11 KJV

. . .

For the word of God is living and powerful, and sharper than any two-edged sword, piercing even to the division of soul and spirit, and of joints and marrow, and is a discerner of the thoughts and intents of the heart.
HEBREWS 4:12 NKJV

. . .

My son, give attention to my words; incline your ear to my sayings. Do not let them depart from your eyes; keep them in the midst of your heart; for they are life to those who find them, and health to all their flesh.
PROVERBS 4:20–22 NKJV

. . .

"So commit yourselves completely to these words of mine. Tie them to your hands as a reminder, and wear them on your forehead. Teach them to your children. Talk about them when you are at home and when you are away on a journey, when you are lying down and when you are getting up again."
DEUTERONOMY 11:18–19 NLT

"As for God, His way is blameless; the word of the LORD is tested; He is a shield to all who take refuge in Him."
2 SAMUEL 22:31 NASB

. . .

All Scripture is inspired by God and profitable for teaching, for reproof, for correction, for training in righteousness; so that the man of God may be adequate, equipped for every good work.
2 TIMOTHY 3:16–17 NASB

. . .

Seek ye out of the book of the LORD, and read: no one of these shall fail, none shall want her mate: for my mouth it hath commanded, and his spirit it hath gathered them.
ISAIAH 34:16 KJV

. . .

Forever, O LORD, Your word is settled in heaven.
PSALM 119:89 NKJV

. . .

But know this first of all, that no prophecy of Scripture is a matter of one's own interpretation, for no prophecy was ever made by an act of human will, but men moved by the Holy Spirit spoke from God.
2 PETER 1:20–21 NASB

The statutes of the LORD are right,
rejoicing the heart; the commandment
of the LORD is pure, enlightening the eyes.
PSALM 19:8 NKJV

• • •

"Do not let this Book of the Law depart from
your mouth; meditate on it day and night, so that
you may be careful to do everything written in it.
Then you will be prosperous and successful."
JOSHUA 1:8 NIV

It is comforting that this Book has indeed manifested
a peculiar ability to speak to the deepest needs and
communicated the Gospel effectively to people of all
different times, places, and customs. The obstacle of
culture cannot make void the power of this Word.
R. C. SPROUL

SELF-CONTROL

Get a grip, will ya? Or, in other words, keep control over yourself—Christians and non-Christians alike are watching to see how you react to the situations of life. Your choice to stand strong in your faith, to resist temptation, or to respond in love will be an encouragement to others. However, a thoughtless word or action can destroy the testimony you're trying to maintain. Who do you really want to be? Much of the answer to that question comes down to self-control.

Whoever has no rule over his own spirit is
like a city broken down, without walls.
PROVERBS 25:28 NKJV

. . .

Or do you not know that the unrighteous will not inherit the
kingdom of God? Do not be deceived; neither fornicators,
nor idolaters, nor adulterers, nor effeminate, nor
homosexuals, nor thieves, nor the covetous, nor drunkards,
nor revilers, nor swindlers, will inherit the kingdom of God.
Such were some of you; but you were washed, but you
were sanctified, but you were justified in the name of the
Lord Jesus Christ and in the Spirit of our God.
1 CORINTHIANS 6:9–11 NASB

. . .

So, dear brothers and sisters, you have no obligation
whatsoever to do what your sinful nature urges you
to do. For if you keep on following it, you will perish.
But if through the power of the Holy Spirit you turn
from it and its evil deeds, you will live.
ROMANS 8:12–13 NLT

. . .

Let your gentleness be known to all men.
The Lord is at hand.
PHILIPPIANS 4:5 NKJV

. . .

For the grace of God that bringeth salvation hath
appeared to all men, teaching us that, denying
ungodliness and worldly lusts, we should live soberly,
righteously, and godly, in this present world; looking for
that blessed hope, and the glorious appearing of the great
God and our Saviour Jesus Christ; who gave himself for us,
that he might redeem us from all iniquity, and purify unto
himself a peculiar people, zealous of good works.
TITUS 2:11–14 KJV

. . . .

But also for this very reason, giving all diligence,
add to your faith virtue, to virtue knowledge, to knowledge
self-control, to self-control perseverance, to perseverance
godliness, to godliness brotherly kindness, and to
brotherly kindness love. For if these things are yours
and abound, you will be neither barren nor unfruitful
in the knowledge of our Lord Jesus Christ.
2 PETER 1:5–8 NKJV

. . . .

For you have been called for this purpose,
since Christ also suffered for you, leaving you
an example for you to follow in His steps, "Who
committed no sin, nor was any deceit found in His
mouth"; and while being reviled, He did not revile in
return; while suffering, He uttered no threats, but kept
entrusting Himself to Him who judges righteously.
1 PETER 2:21–23 NASB

The acts of the sinful nature are obvious:
sexual immorality, impurity and debauchery;
idolatry and witchcraft; hatred, discord, jealousy,
fits of rage, selfish ambition, dissensions, factions
and envy; drunkenness, orgies, and the like. I warn you,
as I did before, that those who live like this will not
inherit the kingdom of God. But the fruit of the Spirit
is love, joy, peace, patience, kindness, goodness,
faithfulness, gentleness and self-control.
GALATIANS 5:19–23 NIV

Moral failure is rarely the result of a blowout;
almost always, it's the result of a slow leak.
GARY OLIVER

SIN

Such a little word. . .such big consequences. Sin is any thought or action that goes against God's will—like that dreaded "fruit incident" in the Garden of Eden that's plagued humanity ever since. Because of our human nature, we will all sin. That, however, is not a license to sin. While God knows we will sin, He has also provided a way of escape so that we can avoid sin's consequences and live to please Him. That way of escape is Jesus.

My dear children, I write this to you so that you will not
sin. But if anybody does sin, we have one who speaks to
the Father in our defense—Jesus Christ, the Righteous
One. He is the atoning sacrifice for our sins, and not
only for ours but also for the sins of the whole world.
1 JOHN 2:1–2 NIV

. . .

This is a faithful saying and worthy of
all acceptance, that Christ Jesus came into
the world to save sinners, of whom I am chief.
1 TIMOTHY 1:15 NKJV

. . .

Knowing this, that our old self was crucified
with Him, in order that our body of sin might
be done away with, so that we would no longer be
slaves to sin; for he who has died is freed from sin.
ROMANS 6:6–7 NASB

. . .

He has removed our rebellious acts as far
away from us as the east is from the west.
PSALM 103:12 NLT

. . .

"For I will be merciful to their unrighteousness, and their
sins and their lawless deeds I will remember no more."
HEBREWS 8:12 NKJV

"Of Him all the prophets bear witness that
through His name everyone who believes
in Him receives forgiveness of sins."
ACTS 10:43 NASB

. . .

But he was wounded for our transgressions,
he was bruised for our iniquities: the chastisement
of our peace was upon him; and with his stripes
we are healed. All we like sheep have gone astray;
we have turned every one to his own way; and the
LORD hath laid on him the iniquity of us all.
ISAIAH 53:5–6 KJV

. . .

. . .who Himself bore our sins in His own body on the
tree, that we, having died to sins, might live for
righteousness—by whose stripes you were healed.
1 PETER 2:24 NKJV

. . .

Your eyes are too pure to approve evil, and You can not
look on wickedness with favor. Why do You look with favor
on those who deal treacherously? Why are You silent when
the wicked swallow up those more righteous than they?
HABAKKUK 1:13 NASB

. . .

If we walk in the Light as He Himself is in the Light,
we have fellowship with one another, and the blood of
Jesus His Son cleanses us from all sin.
1 JOHN 1:7 NASB

Grace and peace to you from God our Father and
the Lord Jesus Christ, who gave himself for our
sins to rescue us from the present evil age,
according to the will of our God and Father.
GALATIANS 1:3–4 NIV

. . .

God's law was given so that all people could see how
sinful they were. But as people sinned more and more,
God's wonderful kindness became more abundant.
ROMANS 5:20 NLT

. . .

"Come now, and let us reason together,"
says the LORD, "though your sins are like scarlet,
they shall be as white as snow; though they
are red like crimson, they shall be as wool."
ISAIAH 1:18 NKJV

Christ's death and resurrection marked the end of sin's
power to control the believer. Just as sin could not control
the Son of God, so it is powerless to control those who
have been placed into Christ through faith.
CHARLES STANLEY

SOBRIETY

"Sobriety" is one of those words you don't hear used a lot these days. But the concept is timeless—it's all about keeping your mind under your own control, and not relinquishing that control to alcohol, drugs, or anything else. If your mind is controlled by anything other than the Holy Spirit, there may be some disastrous consequences. Sobriety is essential in the Christian life.

Wine is a mocker, strong drink a brawler,
and whoever is intoxicated by it is not wise.
PROVERBS 20:1 NASB

. . .

Do not be with heavy drinkers of wine, or with gluttonous
eaters of meat. . . . Do not look on the wine when it is red,
when it sparkles in the cup, when it goes down smoothly;
at the last it bites like a serpent and stings like a viper.
PROVERBS 23:20, 31–32 NASB

. . .

Be sober, be vigilant; because your adversary
the devil walks about like a roaring lion,
seeking whom he may devour.
1 PETER 5:8 NKJV

. . .

Like tangled thorns, and like those who are
drunken with their drink, they are consumed
as stubble completely withered.
NAHUM 1:10 NASB

. . .

So whether you eat or drink or whatever
you do, do it all for the glory of God.
1 CORINTHIANS 10:31 NIV

. . .

Let us walk properly, as in the day,
not in revelry and drunkenness, not in
lewdness and lust, not in strife and envy.
ROMANS 13:13 NKJV

. . .

"How terrible it will be for you who make your
neighbors drunk! You force your cup on them so
that you can gloat over their nakedness and shame."
HABAKKUK 2:15 NLT

. . .

Therefore let us not sleep, as others do, but let us
watch and be sober. For those who sleep, sleep at night,
and those who get drunk are drunk at night.
1 THESSALONIANS 5:6–7 NKJV

. . .

They will eat, but not have enough; they will
play the harlot, but not increase, because they
have stopped giving heed to the LORD. Harlotry,
wine and new wine take away the understanding.
HOSEA 4:10–11 NASB

. . .

Woe unto them that are mighty to drink wine,
and men of strength to mingle strong drink.
ISAIAH 5:22 KJV

"But take heed to yourselves, lest your hearts be weighed down with carousing, drunkenness, and cares of this life, and that Day come on you unexpectedly."
LUKE 21:34 NKJV

. . .

"Now therefore, be careful not to drink wine or strong drink, nor eat any unclean thing."
JUDGES 13:4 NASB

. . .

The acts of the sinful nature are obvious: sexual immorality, impurity and debauchery; idolatry and witchcraft; hatred, discord, jealousy, fits of rage, selfish ambition, dissensions, factions and envy; drunkenness, orgies, and the like. I warn you, as I did before, that those who live like this will not inherit the kingdom of God.
GALATIANS 5:19–21 NIV

. . .

For the grace of God that brings salvation has appeared to all men, teaching us that, denying ungodliness and worldly lusts, we should live soberly, righteously, and godly in the present age, looking for the blessed hope and glorious appearing of our great God and Savior Jesus Christ.
TITUS 2:11–13 NKJV

For the heavy drinker and the glutton will come to
poverty, and drowsiness will clothe one with rags.
PROVERBS 23:21 NASB

. . .

Don't be drunk with wine, because that will ruin your life.
Instead, let the Holy Spirit fill and control you. Then you
will sing psalms and hymns and spiritual songs among
yourselves, making music to the Lord in your hearts.
And you will always give thanks for everything to God
the Father in the name of our Lord Jesus Christ.
EPHESIANS 5:18–20 NLT

. . .

Woe to those who rise early in the morning,
that they may follow intoxicating drink;
who continue until night, till wine inflames them!
ISAIAH 5:11 NKJV

. . .

Who has woe? Who has sorrow? Who has contentions?
Who has complaining? Who has wounds without cause?
Who has redness of eyes? Those who linger long over
wine, those who go to taste mixed wine.
PROVERBS 23:29–30 NASB

It is good neither to eat flesh, nor to drink wine,
nor any thing whereby thy brother stumbleth,
or is offended, or is made weak.

ROMANS 14:21 KJV

· · ·

Do you not know that you are the temple of God
and that the Spirit of God dwells in you? If anyone
defiles the temple of God, God will destroy him.
For the temple of God is holy, which temple you are.

1 CORINTHIANS 3:16–17 NKJV

· · ·

You are all sons of light and sons of day. We are
not of night nor of darkness; so then let us not
sleep as others do, but let us be alert and sober.

1 THESSALONIANS 5:5–6 NASB

It's a great advantage not to
drink among hard drinking people.
F. SCOTT FITZGERALD

TEMPTATION

Have you seen the bumper sticker that says, "I can resist anything but temptation"? It's funny, but it's also pretty accurate. Temptation is strong stuff—why else do you think Satan would use it so much? When you face temptation, remember that Christ Himself was also tempted. If Jesus could be tempted, it stands to reason that there is no sin in being tempted; you sin when you give in to temptation. Jesus fought off Satan's temptation by quoting scripture and remaining faithful to His heavenly Father—just as we should do.

Blessed is a man who perseveres under trial;
for once he has been approved, he will receive the
crown of life which the Lord has promised to those who
love Him. Let no one say when he is tempted, "I am being
tempted by God"; for God cannot be tempted by evil,
and He Himself does not tempt anyone. But each one is
tempted when he is carried away and enticed by his own
lust. Then when lust has conceived, it gives birth to sin;
and when sin is accomplished, it brings forth death.
JAMES 1:12–15 NASB

. . .

"Watch and pray so that you will not fall into temptation.
The spirit is willing, but the body is weak."
MATTHEW 26:41 NIV

. . .

Therefore let him who thinks he stands take heed that
he does not fall. No temptation has overtaken you but
such as is common to man; and God is faithful, who will
not allow you to be tempted beyond what you are able,
but with the temptation will provide the way of escape
also, so that you will be able to endure it.
1 CORINTHIANS 10:12–13 NASB

Great peace have those who love Your law,
and nothing causes them to stumble.
PSALM 119:165 NKJV

. . .

So you see, the Lord knows how to rescue godly
people from their trials, even while punishing the
wicked right up until the day of judgment.
2 PETER 2:9 NLT

. . .

When He came to the place, He said to them,
"Pray that you may not enter into temptation."
LUKE 22:40 NKJV

. . .

For we do not have a high priest who cannot sympathize
with our weaknesses, but One who has been tempted in
all things as we are, yet without sin. Therefore let us draw
near with confidence to the throne of grace, so that we
may receive mercy and find grace to help in time of need.
HEBREWS 4:15–16 NASB

. . .

Though he fall, he shall not be utterly cast down:
for the LORD upholdeth him with his hand.
PSALM 37:24 KJV

"And do not lead us into temptation, but deliver us from evil. For Yours is the kingdom and the power and the glory forever. Amen."
MATTHEW 6:13 NASB

While external circumstances often contribute to our sinning, temptation begins in the heart. Our minds and hearts choose to sin long before we commit the act.
WARREN WIERSBE

THOUGHT LIFE

Your thought life is the most private part of you—who are you, really? It is possible to hide those innermost thoughts from others, but God sees all of them, good or bad. If you struggle with impure thoughts, God is able to clean your mind. Confess your sins and replace those bad thoughts with God's Word. It may take time and effort, but you'll find it's well worth the investment.

Do not conform any longer to the pattern of this world,
but be transformed by the renewing of your mind.
Then you will be able to test and approve what God's
will is—his good, pleasing and perfect will.
ROMANS 12:2 NIV

• • •

I remember the days of old; I meditate on all
Your works; I muse on the work of Your hands.
PSALM 143:5 NKJV

• • •

Evil plans are an abomination to the LORD,
but pleasant words are pure.
PROVERBS 15:26 NASB

• • •

Since you have been raised to new life with Christ,
set your sights on the realities of heaven, where Christ
sits at God's right hand in the place of honor and power.
Let heaven fill your thoughts. Do not think only about
things down here on earth. For you died when Christ died,
and your real life is hidden with Christ in God. And when
Christ, who is your real life, is revealed to the whole
world, you will share in all his glory.
COLOSSIANS 3:1–4

For "who has known the mind of the LORD that he may instruct Him?" But we have the mind of Christ.
1 CORINTHIANS 2:16 NKJV

· · ·

And He said to him, " 'You shall love the LORD your God with all your heart, and with all your soul, and with all your mind.' "
MATTHEW 22:37 NASB

· · ·

Search me, O God, and know my heart: try me, and know my thoughts: And see if there be any wicked way in me, and lead me in the way everlasting.
PSALM 139:23–24 KJV

· · ·

You will keep him in perfect peace, whose mind is stayed on You, because he trusts in You.
ISAIAH 26:3 NKJV

· · ·

"As for you, my son Solomon, know the God of your father, and serve Him with a whole heart and a willing mind; for the LORD searches all hearts, and understands every intent of the thoughts. If you seek Him, He will let you find Him; but if you forsake Him, He will reject you forever."
1 CHRONICLES 28:9 NASB

"The good man brings good things out of the good stored up in his heart, and the evil man brings evil things out of the evil stored up in his heart. For out of the overflow of his heart his mouth speaks."

LUKE 6:45 NIV

. . .

Keep your heart with all diligence,
for out of it spring the issues of life.

PROVERBS 4:23 NKJV

. . .

Create in me a clean heart, O God,
and renew a steadfast spirit within me.

PSALM 51:10 NASB

. . .

For the word of God is full of living power. It is sharper than the sharpest knife, cutting deep into our innermost thoughts and desires. It exposes us for what we really are.

HEBREWS 4:12 NLT

. . .

Examine me, O LORD, and prove me; try my mind and my heart. For Your loving-kindness is before my eyes, and I have walked in Your truth.

PSALM 26:2–3 NKJV

"I, the LORD, search the heart, I test the mind,
even to give to each man according to his ways,
according to the results of his deeds."
JEREMIAH 17:10 NASB

. . .

For from within, out of the heart of men, proceed evil
thoughts, adulteries, fornications, murders, thefts,
covetousness, wickedness, deceit, lasciviousness, an evil
eye, blasphemy, pride, foolishness: All these evil things
come from within, and defile the man.
MARK 7:21–23 KJV

. . .

Let the words of my mouth and the meditation
of my heart be acceptable in Your sight,
O LORD, my strength and my Redeemer.
PSALM 19:14 NKJV

. . .

For those who are according to the flesh set
their minds on the things of the flesh, but those
who are according to the Spirit, the things of
the Spirit. For the mind set on the flesh is death,
but the mind set on the Spirit is life and peace.
ROMANS 8:5–6 NASB

. . .

I will meditate on all Your work and muse on Your deeds.
PSALM 77:12 NASB

Let the wicked forsake his way and the evil man his thoughts. Let him turn to the LORD, and he will have mercy on him, and to our God, for he will freely pardon.
ISAIAH 55:7 NIV

. . .

. . .bringing every thought into captivity to the obedience of Christ.
2 CORINTHIANS 10:5 NKJV

. . .

Throw off your old evil nature and your former way of life, which is rotten through and through, full of lust and deception. Instead, there must be a spiritual renewal of your thoughts and attitudes.
EPHESIANS 4:22–23 NLT

. . .

The peace of God, which surpasses all understanding, will guard your hearts and minds through Christ Jesus.
PHILIPPIANS 4:7 NKJV

. . .

"But seek first His kingdom and His righteousness, and all these things will be added to you."
MATTHEW 6:33 NASB

Thou knowest my downsitting and mine uprising,
thou understandest my thought afar off.
PSALM 139:2 KJV

· · ·

When I was a child, I spoke as a child,
I understood as a child, I thought as a child;
but when I became a man, I put away childish things.
1 CORINTHIANS 13:11 NKJV

· · ·

Finally, brothers, whatever is true, whatever is noble,
whatever is right, whatever is pure, whatever is lovely,
whatever is admirable—if anything is excellent or
praiseworthy—think about such things.
PHILIPPIANS 4:8 NIV

A man's what he thinks about all day long.
RALPH WALDO EMERSON

WISDOM

Know somebody who's smart? Know anybody who's wise? There is a difference. God wants us to be wise—people who properly use their knowledge. The catch is that we can't be wise in our own power. So, as usual, God will provide what we need. The wisdom He expects us to show is free for the asking (see James 1:5).

Love wisdom like a sister; make insight
a beloved member of your family.
PROVERBS 7:4 NLT

* * *

If any of you lacks wisdom, let him ask of God,
who gives to all liberally and without reproach, and it
will be given to him. But let him ask in faith, with no
doubting, for he who doubts is like a wave of the sea
driven and tossed by the wind. For let not that man
suppose that he will receive anything from the Lord;
he is a double-minded man, unstable in all his ways.
JAMES 1:5–8 NKJV

* * *

Who is wise? Let him give heed to these things,
and consider the lovingkindness of the LORD.
PSALM 107:43 NASB

* * *

A wise son maketh a glad father: but a
foolish son is the heaviness of his mother.
PROVERBS 10:1 KJV

* * *

Wisdom and knowledge will be the stability
of your times, and the strength of salvation;
the fear of the LORD is His treasure.
ISAIAH 33:6 NKJV

For the report of your obedience has reached to all;
therefore I am rejoicing over you, but I want you to be
wise in what is good and innocent in what is evil.
ROMANS 16:19 NASB

. . .

Whoever gives heed to instruction prospers, and blessed
is he who trusts in the LORD. The wise in heart are called
discerning, and pleasant words promote instruction.
PROVERBS 16:20–21 NIV

. . .

Those who are wise shall shine like the brightness
of the firmament, and those who turn many to
righteousness like the stars forever and ever.
DANIEL 12:3 NKJV

. . .

But if any of you lacks wisdom, let him
ask of God, who gives to all generously and
without reproach, and it will be given to him.
JAMES 1:5 NASB

. . .

How much better is it to get wisdom than gold! and to
get understanding rather to be chosen than silver!
PROVERBS 16:16 KJV

Let those who are wise understand these things. Let those who are discerning listen carefully. The paths of the LORD are true and right, and righteous people live by walking in them. But sinners stumble and fall along the way.
HOSEA 14:9 NLT

. . .

However, we speak wisdom among those who are mature, yet not the wisdom of this age, nor of the rulers of this age, who are coming to nothing. But we speak the wisdom of God in a mystery, the hidden wisdom which God ordained before the ages for our glory, which none of the rulers of this age knew; for had they known, they would not have crucified the Lord of glory.
1 CORINTHIANS 2:6–8 NKJV

. . .

The teaching of the wise is a fountain of life, to turn aside from the snares of death. Good understanding produces favor, but the way of the treacherous is hard.
PROVERBS 13:14–15 NASB

. . .

"I, wisdom, dwell together with prudence;
I possess knowledge and discretion."
PROVERBS 8:12 NIV

"Therefore everyone who hears these words of Mine and acts on them, may be compared to a wise man who built his house on the rock. And the rain fell, and the floods came, and the winds blew and slammed against that house; and yet it did not fall, for it had been founded on the rock."

MATTHEW 7:24–25 NASB

. . .

Who is a wise man and endued with knowledge among you? Let him shew out of a good conversation his works with meekness of wisdom. But if ye have bitter envying and strife in your hearts, glory not, and lie not against the truth. This wisdom descendeth not from above, but is earthly, sensual, devilish. . . . But the wisdom that is from above is first pure, then peaceable, gentle, and easy to be intreated, full of mercy and good fruits, without partiality, and without hypocrisy.

JAMES 3:13–15, 17 KJV

. . .

He who keeps his command will experience nothing harmful; and a wise man's heart discerns both time and judgment.

ECCLESIASTES 8:5 NKJV

Get wisdom! Get understanding! Do not forget, nor turn away from the words of my mouth. Do not forsake her, and she will preserve you; love her, and she will keep you. Wisdom is the principal thing; therefore get wisdom. And in all your getting, get understanding. Exalt her, and she will promote you; she will bring you honor, when you embrace her. She will place on your head an ornament of grace; a crown of glory she will deliver to you. Hear, my son, and receive my sayings, and the years of your life will be many. I have taught you in the way of wisdom; I have led you in right paths. When you walk, your steps will not be hindered, and when you run, you will not stumble. Take firm hold of instruction, do not let go; keep her, for she is your life.
PROVERBS 4:5–13 NKJV

Wisdom is the right use of knowledge. To know is not to be wise. Many men know a great deal, and are all the greater fools for it. There is no fool so great a fool as a knowing fool. But to know how to use knowledge is to have wisdom.
CHARLES SPURGEON

WITNESSING

Look in the dictionary, and you'll find that the word *witness* can mean "one who has personal knowledge of something." If you're a Christian, you qualify as a witness—someone who knows Jesus Christ, and can tell others about Him. We cross paths with non-Christians every day—and you may be the only Christian that a lost person meets. Be a shining example of Christ in both your words and actions. Because of your testimony, someone may have the privilege of being saved just like you were.

Yet for this reason I found mercy, so that in me
as the foremost, Jesus Christ might demonstrate
His perfect patience as an example for those
who would believe in Him for eternal life.
1 TIMOTHY 1:16 NASB

. . .

"You are the light of the world. A city on a hill cannot
be hidden. Neither do people light a lamp and put it
under a bowl. Instead they put it on its stand, and it gives
light to everyone in the house. In the same way, let your
light shine before men, that they may see your good
deeds and praise your Father in heaven."
MATTHEW 5:14–16 NIV

. . .

Therefore do not be ashamed of the testimony of our
Lord, nor of me His prisoner, but share with me in the
sufferings for the gospel according to the power of God.
2 TIMOTHY 1:8 NKJV

. . .

My brethren, if any among you strays from the truth
and one turns him back, let him know that he who
turns a sinner from the error of his way will save his
soul from death and will cover a multitude of sins.
JAMES 5:19–20 NASB

And have no fellowship with the unfruitful works of darkness, but rather expose them. For it is shameful even to speak of those things which are done by them in secret. But all things that are exposed are made manifest by the light, for whatever makes manifest is light.
EPHESIANS 5:11–13 NKJV

. . .rescuing you from the Jewish people and from the Gentiles, to whom I am sending you, to open their eyes so that they may turn from darkness to light and from the dominion of Satan to God, that they may receive forgiveness of sins and an inheritance among those who have been sanctified by faith in Me.
ACTS 26:17–18 NASB

Preach the word! Be ready in season and out of season. Convince, rebuke, exhort, with all longsuffering and teaching.
2 TIMOTHY 4:2 NKJV

Let the redeemed of the LORD say so, whom He has redeemed from the hand of the adversary.
PSALM 107:2 NASB

But in your hearts set apart Christ as Lord.
Always be prepared to give an answer to everyone
who asks you to give the reason for the hope that
you have. But do this with gentleness and respect.
1 PETER 3:15 NIV

There's no better witness to the
watching world than believers
who stand firm under suffering.
MICHAEL W. SMITH

WORSHIP

Worship isn't only for church. At work, in the car, exercising, whenever—we can be in a constant state of worship, praising God for His goodness. He doesn't expect eloquent or lengthy prayers (in fact, God is probably most pleased with the simplest words—that childlike faith, you know). Wherever you are, whatever you're doing, just express to God your thankfulness for Him.

Come, let us worship and bow down.
Let us kneel before the LORD our maker.
PSALM 95:6 NLT

. . .

"But an hour is coming, and now is, when the
true worshipers will worship the Father in spirit
and truth; for such people the Father seeks to be
His worshipers. God is spirit, and those who
worship Him must worship in spirit and truth."
JOHN 4:23–24 NASB

. . .

Then I saw another angel flying in the midst of
heaven, having the everlasting gospel to preach
to those who dwell on the earth—to every nation,
tribe, tongue, and people—saying with a loud voice,
"Fear God and give glory to Him, for the hour of His
judgment has come; and worship Him who made
heaven and earth, the sea and springs of water."
REVELATION 14:6–7 NKJV

. . .

"You alone are the LORD. You have made the
heavens, the heaven of heavens with all their host,
the earth and all that is on it, the seas and all that
is in them. You give life to all of them and the
heavenly host bows down before You."
NEHEMIAH 9:6 NASB

And Jesus answered and said to him, "Get behind Me, Satan! For it is written, 'You shall worship the LORD your God, and Him only you shall serve.' "
LUKE 4:8 NKJV

. . .

"Then the sovereignty, the dominion and the greatness of all the kingdoms under the whole heaven will be given to the people of the saints of the Highest One; His kingdom will be an everlasting kingdom, and all the dominions will serve and obey Him."
DANIEL 7:27 NASB

. . .

"But the LORD your God you shall fear; and He will deliver you from the hand of all your enemies."
2 KINGS 17:39 NKJV

. . .

"Who shall not fear You, O Lord, and glorify Your name? For You alone are holy. For all nations shall come and worship before You, for Your judgments have been manifested."
REVELATION 15:4 NKJV

Therefore, since we receive a kingdom which cannot be shaken, let us show gratitude, by which we may offer to God an acceptable service with reverence and awe.
HEBREWS 12:28 NASB

. . .

All the nations—and you made each one—
will come and bow before you, Lord;
they will praise your great and holy name.
PSALM 86:9 NLT

. . .

"Do not follow other gods to serve and worship them; do not provoke me to anger with what your hands have made. Then I will not harm you."
JEREMIAH 25:6 NIV

. . .

Ascribe to the LORD the glory due His name;
bring an offering, and come before Him;
worship the LORD in holy array.
1 CHRONICLES 16:29 NASB

Serve the LORD with gladness:
come before his presence with singing.
PSALM 100:2 KJV

• • •

I beseech you therefore, brethren, by the mercies of
God, that you present your bodies a living sacrifice, holy,
acceptable to God, which is your reasonable service.
ROMANS 12:1 NKJV

When we're alone with God, there are no more
distractions to the development of intimacy. It is
just us and Him. The rest of the world must wait.
WELLINGTON BOONE

ZEAL

Do you ever use the word *zeal*? Maybe *passion* is a more common term these days.

Zeal, passion, fervor, enthusiasm. . .call it want you want, the idea is found throughout the Bible. There's the zeal of God toward His people, and of His people back to Him.

Human zeal can be a beautiful thing, a passion for serving God by serving the people around you. That doesn't make you a fanatic—it makes you like Jesus!

For zeal for your house consumes me, and the
insults of those who insult you fall on me.
PSALM 69:9 NIV

• • •

Whatsoever thy hand findeth to do, do it with thy might;
for there is no work, nor device, nor knowledge,
nor wisdom, in the grave, whither thou goest.
ECCLESIASTES 9:10 KJV

• • •

He put on righteousness like a breastplate,
and a helmet of salvation on His head; And He
put on garments of vengeance for clothing
and wrapped Himself with zeal as a mantle.
ISAIAH 59:17 NASB

• • •

Even so you, since you are zealous for
spiritual gifts, let it be for the edification
of the church that you seek to excel.
1 CORINTHIANS 14:12 NKJV

. . .fervent in spirit; serving the Lord.
ROMANS 12:11 KJV

. . .

It is good to be zealously affected
always in a good thing.
GALATIANS 4:18 KJV

. . .

. . .while we look forward with hope to that wonderful day
when the glory of our great God and Savior, Jesus Christ,
will be revealed. He gave his life to free us from every kind
of sin, to cleanse us, and to make us his very own people,
totally committed to doing good deeds.
TITUS 2:13–14 NLT

. . .

God is not unjust; he will not forget your work and
the love you have shown him as you have helped his
people and continue to help them. We want each
of you to show this same diligence to the very end,
in order to make your hope sure.
HEBREWS 6:10–11 NIV

As many as I love, I rebuke and chasten:
be zealous therefore, and repent.
REVELATION 3:19 KJV

If it doesn't mean anything to you,
it won't mean anything to God.
JENTEZEN FRANKLIN